Jack O'Connell
Seattle
26 December 1978

Enter the
Irish-American

Enter the Irish-American

EDWARD WAKIN

Thomas Y. Crowell Company
ESTABLISHED 1834 / NEW YORK

Designed by Ingrid Beckman

Manufactured in the United States of America

Library of Congress Cataloging in Publication Data
Wakin, Edward.
 Enter the Irish-American.

 Includes index.
 1. Irish Americans—History. I. Title.
E184.I6W3   973'.04'9162   72-7582
ISBN 0–690-26722-3

10 9 8 7 6 5 4 3 2 1

To Eleanor

Books by Edward Wakin

A Lonely Minority: The Modern Story of Egypt's Copts
The Catholic Campus
At the Edge of Harlem: Portrait
  of a Middle-Class Negro Family
The De-Romanization of the
  American Catholic Church (with J. F. Scheuer)
Controversial Conversations with Catholics
Black Fighting Men in U.S. History
We Were Never Their Age (with James DiGiacomo)
The Battle for Childhood
Careers in Communications
Children Without Justice
Enter the Irish-American

Contents

Enter the
Irish-American

Introduction

THEY WERE THE FIRST LARGE WAVE of immigrants to land in nineteenth-century America, arriving poor and desperate, uprooted strangers in a strange world.

They fought to belong, to survive, and to get ahead as would all newcomers to America. They endured the hardships and insults that beset all immigrants. They were mostly country folk and they became mostly city people. They were at the bottom of the social ladder and they struggled upwards.

They are the Irish—more than four and a quarter million of them who came to the United States between 1820 and 1920. This story of their experiences is told largely in their own words or in the words of others who observed and set down what it meant to be Irish in America.

Personal accounts describe why they left home, what they found on arriving, and how they worked and worshipped, played, politicked, and paraded, suffered, prospered, and

1

fought for both Ireland and America. Many voices joined in—from railhand to politician, from maid to monsignor, from saloonkeeper to disdainful Yankee. Contemporary letters, diaries, newspapers, magazines, and books tell the story first-hand.

While this is an Irish tale, it also constitutes the story of all newcomers to "A Nation of Immigrants"—as President John F. Kennedy called the United States when he placed all immigrant experiences in their historical context:

> The continuous immigration of the nineteenth and early twentieth centuries was thus central to the whole American faith. It gave every old American a standard by which to judge how far he had come and every new American a realization of how far he might go. It reminded every American, old and new, that change is the essence of life, and that American society is a process, not a conclusion. The abundant resources of this land provided the foundation for a great nation. But only people could make the opportunity a reality. Immigration provided the human resources. More than that, it infused the nation with a commitment to far horizons and new frontiers, and thereby kept the pioneer spirit of American life, the spirit of equality and of hope, always alive and strong. "We are the heirs of all time," wrote Herman Melville, "and with all nations we divide our inheritance." [1]

Thus, to recall the Irish immigrant story is to recall also the story of America, as historian Oscar Handlin has pointed out: "Once I thought to write a history of the immigrants in America. Then I discovered that the immigrants *were* American history." [2]

The experiences of the Irish in America were often typical of other immigrants, but in some ways, also unique. They were unlike any other group in their militant manner and the degree to which they "converted" America to Irish ways. They became celebrated as the "Fighting Irish" after being castigated as rowdy and riotous. And they persuaded the entire country to join them in celebrating the particularly-Irish St. Patrick's Day—an annual success achieved by no other nationality.

The Irish determined and directed the development of popular government in American cities and they were in the forefront of the nascent labor movement. They transformed their beleaguered church into an expression of their piety, pride, and power. They did not apologize for their ethnic identity; they advertised it. Today, in the final quarter of the twentieth century, a resurgence of ethnic identity among all immigrant groups would seem to recertify the Irish pattern— which was to be both Irish and American. (In the 1970's, a well-known Slovak-American intellectual, Michael Novak, has gained respectful attention by arguing that American "ethnics" are unmeltable.)

The Irish were also outrageous as were no other immigrants. They formed their own nation within the nation, even to running up the Irish nationalist flag on New York's Union Square or mounting an invasion of Canada from American soil. Suddenly, in 1866, Buffalo, New York, was inundated with Irish-Americans arriving from all directions. They were coming for the invasion of Canada under their own Secretary of War as part of the abiding determination to free Ireland. (Irish-Americans invaded Canada not once but twice.)

As the Irish immigrant experience unfolded between 1820 and 1920, the Irish themselves and those who "experienced" them provided a running commentary. At times, it seems as though they were not talking about the same people. Like life itself, the Irish experience has had many sides and many derivations, sometimes complicated and contradictory.

There were many different Irishmen with real and fancied traits; many things could be said about them, and usually were. Reactions were plentiful, indifference rare. So it is not possible to present the Irish story without a recurring chorus of praise and abuse.

In 1841, a sympathetic view: "How gallantly, indeed, do Irish wit, and cheerfulness, and hospitality, and patriotism ride on the wreck of individual hopes, and sparkle through the very waves of adversity!" [3]

In 1851, an Irishman writing home: The Irish position "is one of shame and poverty. . . . 'My master is a great tyrant,' said a negro lately, 'he treats me as badly as if I was a *common Irishman.*' " [4]

In 1854, Orestes Brownson, celebrated convert to Catholicism: "Out of these narrow lanes, dirty streets, damp cellars, and suffocating garrets, will come forth some of the noblest sons of our country, whom she will delight to own and honor." [5]

In 1854, an English traveller in the United States: The Irish "soon acquire the sentiments of self-respect common to the American character" . . . they become "more Americanized than the Americans." [6]

In 1863, a prominent New Yorker: "I am sorry to find that England is right about the lower class of Irish. They are brutal, base, cruel, cowards, and as insolent as base. . . . my own theory is that St. Patrick's campaign against the snakes is a Popish delusion. They perished of biting the Irish people." [7]

In 1864, from a travelling Irish author: "thousands of my countrymen at this time fill with dignity and invulnerable fidelity, various situations of trust and emolument in the land of their adoption. . . ." [8]

In 1868, the *Chicago Post*: "Scratch a convict or a pauper, and the chances are that you tickle the skin of an Irish Catholic."

On October 29, 1884, that ill-advised and infamous statement of a Presbyterian clergyman to a presidential candidate visiting New York City: "We are Republicans, and don't propose to leave our party and identify ourselves with the party whose antecedents have been RUM, ROMANISM, and REBELLION."

In 1896, George Bernard Shaw: "Of all the tricks which the Irish nation have played on the slow-witted Saxon, the most outrageous is the palming off on him of the imaginary Irishman of romance. The worst of it is that when a spurious type gets into literature, it strikes the imagination of boys and girls. They form themselves by playing up to it; and thus the unsubstantial fancies of the novelists and music-hall song-writers of one generation are apt to become the unpleasant and mischievous realities of the next." [9]

Of course, there is no day like St. Patrick's Day for bringing forth the heights of commentary by, for, and of Irishmen. And, of course, the mythical "Mr. Dooley," created by Finley Peter Dunne, is hard to surpass. Said he in a turn-of-the-century conversation one St. Patrick's Day, after noting that being Irish is an "incur'ble habit":

> ". . . Annyhow 'tis a good thing to be an Irishman because people think that all an Irishman does is to laugh without a reason an' fight without an objick. But ye an' I, Hinnissy, know these things ar-re on'y our diversions. It's a good thing to have people size ye up wrong, whin they're got ye'er measure ye're in danger."
>
> "Sometimes I think we boast too much," said Mr. Hennessy.
>
> "Well," said Mr. Dooley, "it's on'y on Pathrick's Day we can hire others to blow our horns f'r us." [10]

It was that way with the Irish in the nineteenth and early twentieth centuries. They did a good deal of talking about themselves, and so did others. There was no ignoring the Irish; they were the most public of immigrants. There are plentiful accounts of their experiences and probably too many polemics *pro* and *con*. It is revealing to hear how they tell it from their own experiences and how others (friendly and hostile) saw them add the hyphen to their identity as Irish-Americans. While the hyphenated identity belonged to all immigrants, the Irish added a third dimension that played an emotional part in their American experience: hatred of England running along-side love of Erin and loyalty to America.

In the process, the accounts from all sides weave a colorful tapestry of hope and hardship, success and failure, laughter and tears, hostility and saving grace. All in all, a hell of a lot of people living and telling one hell of a story.

I

Heavy Hearts and High Hopes

IN THE EARLY PART of the nineteenth century, the U.S. consul in Dublin reported that "the principal freight from Ireland to the United States consists of Passengers." They became the oppressed island's primary export as able-bodied sons and daughters left a beloved homeland of unrewarding toil and historic trouble.

Historian Carl Wittke has commented that "it would be difficult to find another country where the causes for large-scale emigration were so compelling as in the Ireland of the eighteenth and nineteenth centuries." [1] For the Irish were suffering in mind, body, and soul. Politically, they raged at the rule of the British who added alien faith to alien domination, oppressive laws to military conquest. The country was racked by poverty, illiteracy, low wages, high rents, unemployment, unsuccessful rebellions, and recurring famines. Three-fourths

7

of the land was owned by English landlords who, it was noted, "planted tenants as their most profitable crop."

Irish emigration became less a leave-taking in hope than a flight in desperation. The emigration has been singled out as the one migratory movement in modern history that encompassed a major part of a country's population and led directly to a population decline. The four million nineteenth-century emigrants reduced Ireland from a country of eight and a half million in 1846 to four and a half million in 1901. In proportion to total population, no other country lost more of its sons and daughters by emigration. (As early as 1860, the U.S. census commissioner reported that for every Irish immigrant in the country only five remained at home compared with ratios of one to 33 for Germany and one to 34 for Norway.)

As much as they hated to go, the Irish were accumulating good reasons to leave. Since the first incursions in the twelfth century, the English had been absorbed in the task of bringing the Irish to heel. The two islands of England and Ireland—"divided by nature but united by force"—were in a state of confrontation in which advantage rested entirely with the English. The Irish experienced what were, in effect, unending English "invasions" because the English conquest was never complete. The Irish either rebelled or were rebellious and they suffered for it.

The suffering was encoded in the infamous Penal Laws, which sociologist (and Irish-American) Andrew M. Greeley has called "the most savage, the most repressive legislation that the modern world has ever seen." [2] Dating back to Elizabethan times, these laws were carried to oppressive extremes after the triumph of William of Orange at the Battle of Boyne in 1690. They stripped the Irish of power and tried to deprive them of their pride as well.

To be English and Anglican was everything; to be Irish and Catholic, almost nothing at all. The four out of five Irish who were Catholics could not vote, sit in Parliament, serve on a jury, teach school, enter a university, work for the government, carry a gun, manufacture or sell books. Nor could they buy land from a Protestant, hire more than two apprentices, or even own a horse worth more than five guineas.

Irish Catholics even had to pay tithes to support the detested Anglican Church. Their own chapels could not have belfries, towers, or steeples. Their public crosses were destroyed. Their priests had to register their names and parishes under penalty of branding and were not permitted to leave the confines of their parishes. They could not—under pain of death—perform a wedding ceremony between a Catholic and a Protestant.

The laws were fussy and detailed as well. Anyone discovering a Catholic schoolmaster earned a reward of ten pounds. Anyone finding a Catholic riding a horse worth more than five pounds could compel him to sell it for five pounds. No Catholic could hold a lease for more than 30 years and, upon his death, his land was parceled out to all his sons—unless the eldest became a Protestant. In that case, he acquired all the land.

Reformed, revised, and enforced with variable severity, these Draconian laws survived into the twentieth century. The spirit of the Penal Code was unabashedly summarized by Lord Chancellor Bowen: "The law does not suppose any such person to exist as an Irish Roman Catholic."

Faced with a high-handed, repressive legal system, the Irish used wit, double-talk, and *blarney* to compensate for weakness. On one side, the powerful invader; on the other, the witty evader. As far back as the sixteenth century, the Lord of Blarney had set an example when Queen Elizabeth demanded that he renounce any ancestral right to his land and acknowledge instead that he held it by virtue of a grant from the Crown. He evaded the demand "with fair words and soft speech" until Elizabeth was heard to complain, "This is all Blarney. What he says he never means." Thus the meaning of *blarney* as soft deception and the tradition that kissing the stone at Blarney Castle sets eloquence upon the lips.

Irish suffering and English oppression were centered around the soil, from which landlords drew enormous wealth and the farmers a scanty existence. Of Ireland's 15 million cultivable acres, the British government had taken 12 million, leaving one-seventh of the land to the four-fifths of the population that was Irish Catholic. Looking at the economic structure from the top down, less than one percent of the total population owned 80 percent of the land (as late as 1869). Below these landlords were leaseholders, mainly Protestants; they were 2.5 percent of the population and held the land in perpetuity. Next came the middlemen who rented land and then sublet in smaller units to tenant farmers. The latter formed the base of the crushing socioeconomic pyramid of poverty.

Tenant farmers were divided into annual tenants; cottiers who lived in poor cottages and cultivated a patch of land; and, finally, agricultural laborers. Life on the Irish farm was as precarious as it was meager. Writing in the final years of the eighteenth century, Arthur Young, an English expert on Ireland, reported: "A landlord in Ireland can scarcely invent an order which a servant, labourer or cottier dares to refuse to execute. Nothing satisfies him but an unlimited submission. Disrespect or any thing tending towards sauciness he may punish with his cane or his horsewhip with the most perfect security; a poor man would have his bones broke if he offered to lift his hand in his own defense." [3]

As noted by an old Irish woman: "We had to squeeze the seeds and eat the hearts out of the rotten potatoes in order to make up the rent for the landlord." Another observer reported that landlords assured him that cottiers would feel "honoured" to have their wives and daughters summoned to the bed of their master—"a mark of slavery which proves the oppression under which such people must live."

The landlord supplied only the land; the farmer had to

provide everything else himself, including all buildings, maintenance, and improvements. Each time the lease was up, the farmer had to pay an even higher rent if his own labors had made the land more valuable. Or he could be ousted if "grabbers" came along and offered a higher rent for the land. Historian George Potter quotes an old Irishman in Mullingar who recalled this saying: "Let any man go down to hell and open an Irishman's heart there; the first thing writ across it was land." Then the old man summarized the way "grabbers," middle men, and landlords operated in the triangle of land oppression:

> The landlord would take the grabber as his tenant and let the unfortunate man who made the holding worth grabbing to the grabber go without any compensation. But more and more money was the objective of the Irish landlord no matter what source it came from. The grabbers and the middle men were the real bane to the Irish peasant farmer. The landlords in themselves were not so bad nor could be so bad without the aid of the grabbers and the middle man.[4]

The typical family lived in a cramped hut whose walls were made of mud mixed with some stones and whose roof of boughs and turf was hardly five feet above the ground. On a dirt floor, man and beast slept huddled together. A German traveller in 1843 called the Irish the poorest people in Europe. Wellington, the "Iron Duke," commented sadly on the plight of his countrymen: "There never was a country in which poverty existed to so great a degree as it exists in Ireland."

The shortage of land and the tripling of Ireland's population between 1779 and 1841 squeezed the Irish peasants, whose lives had been marginal to begin with. The potato literally separated them from starvation; in the best of times, the Irish peasant survived mainly on potatoes, supplemented by milk and occasionally by fish. Needing one-third the acreage of wheat, the potato could be grown without difficulty and stored readily. Its seed was cheap, its planting simple, its harvesting easy. In *Reflections on the Subject of Emigration*, Matthew Carey, an early nineteenth-century Irish-American who prospered in Philadelphia as a book publisher and distributor, noted that the potato constituted "three-fourths of the sustenance of nine-tenths of the laboring classes in Ireland. Thousands do not partake of animal food more than once a year." [5]

When a Poor Inquiry Commission reported to the British Parliament in what was described as "guarded language," this picture of Ireland, during a time of "comparative plenty" prior to the Great Famine of the late 1840's, emerged:

> . . . it is impossible for the able-bodied, in general, to provide against sickness or the temporary absence of employment, or against old age, or the destitution of their widows and children, in the contingent event of their own premature decease. A great portion of them are insufficiently provided at any time with the commonest necessaries of life. Their habitations are wretched hovels; several of a family sleep together upon straw or upon the bare ground, sometimes with a blanket, sometimes even without so much to cover them. Their food commonly consists of dry potatoes; and with these they are at times so scantily supplied as to be obliged to stint themselves to one spare meal in the day. There are instances of persons being driven by hunger to seek sustenance in wild herbs. They sometimes get a herring, or a little milk; but they never get meat, except at Christmas, Easter, or Shrove tide. . . . The wives and children of many are occasionally obliged to beg; they do so reluctantly and with shame, and in general go to a distance from home, that they may not be known.[6]

An Irish member of the British Parliament, William Smith O'Brien, reminded his colleagues in 1840 that it was "impossible to exaggerate the condition of the labouring classes" in Ireland. The "industrious labourer" was "frequently compelled to live, with his family, upon a diet of potatoes, without milk, unprovided with such clothing as decency requires, and sheltered in a hovel wholly unfit for the residence of man." O'Brien then warned, in a grimly prophetic vein, that if the Irishman's meager patch of land should fail to yield its crop of potatoes, he would be "reduced to that absolute extremity of want, which may be properly designated as starvation."

Since the Irish lived from year to year on the potato, each year's crop was watched with hope and apprehension. The year 1844 yielded "a very plentiful crop," according to contemporary accounts, and the early potato harvesting in September of the following year produced optimism. But during the main harvest in December of 1845, the Irish peasant went out to gather potatoes and returned in despair. The precious potato was diseased, rotting in the ground or almost immediately after harvest.

In 1846, optimism returned, for the Irish always said that a bad crop was followed by an abundant one. In July, Father Theobald Mathew, the famous Irish Temperance leader, in travelling from Cork to Dublin, saw the "plant blooming in all the luxuriance of an abundant harvest." Travelling back five days later, he found "one wide waste of putrefying vegetation." The Irish sat at the edge of dead potato patches, weeping as for the death of a loved one.

The blight which decimated the potato struck with full force in the years 1846, 1847, and 1848. In the five years from 1847 to 1851, a million people died from starvation and disease. It was, Lord John Russell told the British House of Commons on January 25, 1847, "a famine of the thirteenth century acting upon the population of the nineteenth."

A nineteenth-century Irish summary of what happened in the Great Famine noted: "The weekly returns of the dead were like the bulletin of a fierce campaign. As the end of the year approached, villages and rural districts, which had been prosperous and populous a year before, were desolate. In some places the loss amounted to half the resident population."

British historian Cecil Woodham-Smith quotes the painful recollections of a woman who lived in Ireland as a young girl during the famine years:

> I can recollect being awakened in the early morning by a strange noise, like the croaking or chattering of many birds. Some of the voices were hoarse and almost extinguished by the faintness of famine; and on looking out of the window I recollect seeing the garden and the field in front of the house completely darkened by a population of men, women and children, squatting in rags; uncovered skeleton limbs protruding everywhere from their wretched clothing, and clamorous though faint voices uplifted for food and in pathetic remonstrance against the inevitable delay in providing what was given them from the house every morning. I recollect too, when walking through the lanes and villages, the strange morbid famine smell in the air, the sign of approaching death, even in those who were still dragging out a wretched existence.[7]

In December, 1846, after cholera had added epidemic to famine, a visitor wrote a letter to the Duke of Wellington, describing the dreadful sight to be seen on entering a cabin in the apparently deserted village of Skibbereen:

> . . . six famished and ghastly skeletons, to all appearance dead, huddled in a corner, their sole covering what seemed to be a ragged horse cloth, and their wretched legs hanging about, naked above the knees. I approached in horror and found by a low moaning that they were alive, they were in fever—four children, a woman and what had once been a man. . . . In a few minutes I was surrounded by at least 200 of such phantoms, such frightful spectres as no words can describe. By far the greater number were delirious either from famine or fever. . . . Within 500 yards of the Cavalry Station at Skibbereen, the dispensary doctor found seven wretches lying, unable to move, under the same cloak—one had been dead many hours, but the others were unable to move, either themselves or the corpse.[8]

An Englishman, sent by the Society of Friends to report on

conditions in western Ireland during the fall of 1847, was struck by "wonder"—"not that the people died, but that they lived." He attributed this to "the long apprenticeship in want" which the Irish endured and to their lovely, touching charity." What little they had was shared with starving neighbors.

Entering the town of Westport, he found "a strange and fearful sight" that resembled a city devastated by war. Townspeople wandered about in a daze, aimlessly, with stunned expressions. At the inn, where the road engineer and pay clerks were headquartered, men crowded around, begging for work. At the poor house, "a mob of starved, almost naked, women" pleaded hysterically for soup tickets.

The Englishman's report struggled for words to express what he had seen in town after town—"men gaunt and haggard, stamped with the livid mark of hunger" . . . "children crying with pain" from hunger . . . women "too weak to stand" . . . laborers walking five to seven miles to work, eating one meal of gruel one day, two the next, some of them working until they fell over their tools, a "slow death" that merely enabled them "to endure for a little longer the disease of hunger." [9]

Anyone who went to see what was taking place in Ireland was stunned by the human suffering, impressed by the will to survive, and, subsequently, haunted by the looks on the faces of Irish peasants. An American evangelist, Mrs. Nicholson, exclaimed, "Good God! Have mercy on poor Ireland." She remembered men crowded into a square, hoping to find work the next morning. Some had walked fifteen miles without eating and with no hope of eating that day. They stood around, waiting, each with his spade, silent, hungry, weary. Mrs. Nicholson could only add: "Their dress and their desponding looks told too well the tale of their suffering." [10]

Contemporary letters to the Illustrated London News depicted the frightful process of dying during the Great Famine and the nightmare of seeing it take place. In one cabin, the wife "some time dead," the father survived with his two children "on a miserable bed, some scanty covering thrown over them, but destitute of clothes; one child was so weak from hunger that he had difficulty even raising himself for the purpose of shewing his emaciated limbs." A laborer sat with his wife and two children "round a bit of fire," with a third child lying dead in its cradle and the family unable to provide a coffin. A police patrol approached a cottage where an unsteady light flickered to find a father and son lying dead, while the survivors, who could not afford a candle, tried to keep a light going with straw pulled from the thatch. One witness told of building a coffin with movable sides so bodies could be brought to the cemetery wrapped in calico bags. He added that he had "just sent this to bring the remains of a poor creature to the grave, who having been turned out of the only shelter she had—a miserable hut—perished the night before last in a quarry; she was found with some flax around her, lying dead." [11]

No Irishman would argue with the definition of his country, in 1849, as "a ruined proprietary, a fugitive tenantry, a destitute people, and a desolate land." And he would bitterly affirm the judgment of the Irish revolutionary John Mitchel who complained of the "very prevalent feeling" in the landlord class at the time that "the people of Ireland ought not to be fed" by the grain produced in the country and that "it is desirable to get rid of a couple of millions of them . . . taking advantage of the panic which is driving the people away." [12] A year after this bitter observation, Mitchel became a leading figure in the abortive rebellion of 1848 and was banished from Ireland to America where he continued to demonstrate his passion for "the fair hills of holy Ireland."

The Great Famine transformed the steadily increasing stream of Irish emigrants into a flood. In 1816 and 1817, from 6,000 to 9,000 sailed for America, the total doubling in 1818. In the early 1830's, the total went over 65,000; in 1842 over

90,000. Cargoes of timber and cotton were being sent to Ireland and human cargoes shipped back on the return voyage. With the onslaught of the Famine in 1846, the number of emigrants was ten times that of 1816 and reached 196,000 in 1847. In a population of eight and a half million, more than one and three-quarter million emigrated between 1846 and 1854, with the overwhelming majority going to the United States.

In the emigrant combination of courage, hope, and desperation, the latter dominated during the Great Famine. Indeed, a mood of panic prevailed. For example, in just the two months of March and April, 1847, it was estimated that some villages in Galway lost almost one-third of their inhabitants. An official report noted: "All who are able are leaving the country." A relief committee watched as emigrants boarded ships for a dreaded winter crossing (spring and fall had been the usual departure times) and reported that "there was nothing but joy at their escape, as from a doomed land." A newspaper of the time told of what members of one group said as they boarded ship—"all we want is to get out of Ireland. . . . we must be anywhere than here."

Even those free of the ravages of the Famine shared the mood of desperation. John O'Donovan, a scholarly librarian of the time who was not suffering as were the peasants, wrote in 1848 that he was "sick" of Ireland. Renowned for his love of Ireland and things Irish, O'Donovan still proclaimed, in correspondence cited by Harvard professor Oscar Handlin, that he "would leave Ireland with a clear conscience," indeed leave it "exultingly, retire among the Backwoods of America." He felt ready to "move into the deserts of the western world there to learn a RUDE but STURDY civilization that knows not slavery or hunger." [13]

There was not only the *push* to emigrate. There was the *pull* of America that had been generated by reports from earlier immigrants. For, as a nineteenth-century Irish bull would have it, "the only place in Ireland where a man can make a fortune is in America." Taking a long view of Irish emigration and its motives, a thoughtful student of the process has concluded that *push* and *pull* were "inextricably intertwined in a myriad-threaded pattern of personal choices and desires." [14] Ireland disappointed, and America beckoned—particularly in the "Amerikay letther."

Letters from America beckoned those at home to follow the emigrants through "the golden door." Truly, America was a land of opportunity, the letters said time and again, but not without telling everyone to expect to work hard, very hard. These letters rippled through the countryside, and not only because of the number of individual families who received them. (An estimated one out of two Irish families received a letter from America during the single year of 1845.) Each letter was a ritualized social event in an Irish village, spreading its influence outward from the emigrant's own family.

Since illiteracy was high, the ritual required that "The Scholar" be fetched to read the letter. The family gathered round, friends were invited in. The group clustered around the letter, each with an opinion on how to open the letter without damaging the contents. An old Irish schoolmaster recalled the moment of opening, while waiting for "The Scholar" to arrive and after spotting an "American Ticket" (American money) inside: "Not a breath escapes while this operation is being performed. Soon fold after fold of the enclosed manuscript is opened. The last one is being turned up and alas! between hope and despair the 'Ticket' appears. There is something in it, whatever it is. This part of the letter, the pearl as it may be called—is taken in charge by the old woman who opens her long cloth purse . . . and in the innermost . . . cavity the American Eagles find a safe retreat." [15] Then "The Scholar" arrives and proceeds to read the letter to an enraptured audience, taking care to keep the purely personal items for the family's ears only.

The letters were warm, eloquent, spirited, personal, and constituted a loving embrace, often beginning with this typical opening: "Dear Father and Mother, I take this favorable opportunity to write these few lines hoping the arrival of this letter finds you in good health as it leaves me at present, thanks be to God for his kind mercies to us all. . . ." [16] The letters, besides reporting favorably on life and opportunity in America, would beckon family members and friends, even set forth plans for bringing them over. The recurrent themes were the opportunities for work, for abundant food (and drink), and for holding your head high. There was scarcely room for doubt on hearing the claims of these letters, for they commonly contained dramatic proof to an impoverished peasantry. Often enclosed was the first-hand testimony of hard cash.

Writing to a sister in County Clare, an Irish woman noted in an 1846 letter that "it would give me greate pleasure to think that you Come here, for i think you would do verry well in this Country. . . . And my sister bridget do what she can to come here. Let my sister Ellen know that she would get 5 shillings to 6 for making one dress here; and if she could possibly come here Let me know. . . ." [17] Ten years before, a County Limerick man wrote to his father from a farm in Ohio that "a poor man in Ireland could not do better than come here, for it is the truth of a good country." John Doyle wrote to his wife from New York that life in America was free from "visits from tax gatherers, constables, or soldiers" and that everyone is "at liberty to act and speak as he likes . . . to slander and damn government, abuse public men in their office to their faces, wear your hat in court and smoke a cigar while speaking to a judge." [18]

Another emigrant reported that he ate every day as he would eat only at Christmas in Ireland, adding: "Any man may speak what is on his mind without the least fear. If a man will work, he need never go hungry." [19] Or in another letter: "Give my very kind love to Father, and tell him if he was here he could soon kill himself by drinking if he thought proper." [20] A French traveller in the United States told of a recently-arrived Irishman who showed his employer the letter he was writing home. "But, Patrick," said the employer, "why do you say that you have meat three times a week, when you have it three times a day?" "Why is it?" replied Pat. "It is because they wouldn't believe me, if I told them so." [21]

Able-bodied men and women were responding to the lure of America in such numbers that one observer labeled the situation in Ireland as "survival of the unfittest." Between 1850 and 1887, two-thirds of the emigrants were 15 to 35 years of age; after that, the proportion rose above four-fifths. Moreover, due partly to the demand for Irish women as domestic servants, women as well as men were leaving in large numbers—unlike other immigrant groups from continental Europe, where male immigrants predominated. Almost half of all Irish emigrants were coming from six of Ireland's 32 counties: Cork, Kerry, Tipperary, Limerick, Galway, and Mayo, all of them predominantly Catholic and most likely to feel the English yoke.

Thus, emigration became part of the Irish way of life during the nineteenth and early twentieth centuries. One observer noted that children were brought up "with the idea of probably becoming emigrants." Indeed, it became a habit in a country strongly wedded to its habits.

II

To a Far Distant Shore

FOR THE IRISH, emigration had the finality of death, a departure without return. Emigrants left for a permanent home in the United States; even a return visit did not seem like a serious possibility. The shattering finality of it struck both individual and family with the impact of the major events of Irish country life: birth, marriage, death. Most of all, death.

Sad ballads were filled with *farewells*—"Farewell ye green hills and verdant valleys" . . . "Farewell dear Erin, fare thee well" . . . "So farewell, I can no longer dwell at home" . . . "A long farewell, my comrade boys". . . . Or as "The Emigrant's Farewell" said it, in the Boston *Pilot* of August 16, 1862:

> Farewell to thee, Erin mavourneen,
>   Thy valleys I'll tread never more;
> This heart that now bleeds for thy sorrows,

Will waste on a far distant shore.
Thy green sods lie cold on my parents,
A cross marks the place of their rest,—
The wind that moans sadly above them,
Will waft their poor child to the West.

In the Irish countryside, from which the great majority of emigrants came, death provided the most important ceremonies, the most dramatic manifestations of community life. In the wake and funeral, as anthropologist Conrad Arensberg described them, the Irish countrymen became involved in a "re-enactment, both solemn and gay, of their sentiments about their fellows and about their view of life and death and destiny." [1] As a kind of death, departure for the United States called forth what became known as the "American wake." In a nineteenth-century notebook, a County Mayo man noted that it had all the characteristics of a wake, "though not of a dead person, but of a living one, who next day would be sailing for the promised land."

For the emigrant, it was like attending his own funeral. The "wake" lasted through the night before leaving, drawing together family, friends, and neighbors to provide emotional support and sympathy. The emigrant would dance a last step for mother and father or sing a favorite ballad. Advice would be freely given, information compared on the New World, requests made to contact a cousin in New York or a brother in Boston.

In the characteristic Irish way, merriment was mixed with mourning. Partying was blended with prayer, good cheer with sadness. There were drinking, dancing, singing—an Irish version of the stiff upper lip. As the older folks sat in a circle around the hearth, music poured forth from fiddle or melodeon and young men and women danced jigs, reels, and versions of Irish step-dancing. In between the dances, songs were sung, drinks drunk, laughter and good cheer spread about.

At the moment of departure, those "last embraces were terrible to see," as described by an eyewitness in the mid-nineteenth century. Even "worse were the kissings and the claspings of the hands during the long minutes that remained. . . . the wringing of hands . . . the wailings. . . . Still, there it was, the pain and the passion: and the shrill united cry, when the [horse] car moved on, rings in our ears, and long will ring when we hear of emigration." [2]

After emigrants left their parents at the doorway, younger family members and friends accompanied them to the railroad station or a particular crossroads. It was a funereal procession leading away from home. If the final leave-taking took place at the railway station, parents would have to be pulled away from departing children. One contemporary onlooker described gray-haired peasants clinging so desperately to their sons and daughters "that only the utmost force of three or four friends could tear them asunder." Train attendants had to fight off the crowd so the train could move out. Then, those remaining behind lingered by the side of the track for a final glimpse of those who were going for good.

A view from the shore was provided by an Irishman who watched from an island off the coast of Kerry: "the bright May morning with the summer sun shining in the heavens, the birds singing in the hedges, and the cuckoo's call echoing in their ears, as the sad procession wended their way down to the emigrant ship—men, women, and children—the very old and the very young—filling the clear summer air with their wails and lamentations." [3]

On a later occasion, an Irish political fugitive watched from a ship's deck as the sun set over Ireland, sharing the feelings of all Irishmen and women leaving Ireland forever. John Boyle O'Reilly was following a circuitous route from court-martial for nationalistic plotting while a member of the Tenth Hussars, to a penal colony in Australia, to escape in an American whaling ship, and, finally, to exile in America. As an Irish-

American, he became a celebrated lecturer, acclaimed literary figure and influential editor of the *Boston Pilot*. Two months after arriving, he recalled in a January 1870 lecture his last look at Ireland:

> Ireland was there, under the sun; but under the dark cloud also. The rays of golden glory fell down from behind the dark cloud—fell down like God's pity on the beautiful, tear-stained face of Ireland—fell down on the dear familiar faces of my old home, on the hill, the wood, the river, lighting them all once more with the same heaven-tint that I loved to watch long ago. Oh! how vividly did that long ago rise up before me then! the happy home, the merry playmates, the faces, the voices of dear ones who are there still, and the hallowed words of dearest ones who are dead,—down on all fell the great glory of the setting sun, lighting that holy spot that I might never see, a mother's grave, and lighting the heart with sorrow-shaded devotion. . . .

Whether the Irish left before or during the Great Famine, or in 1855 (when the flood of emigration subsided to 78,000), or at the end of the nineteenth and the beginning of the twentieth century, they had a similar set of bittersweet recollections. For Irish country life was unchanging. The land, the home, the church, and the socializing framework warmed and worried them in a constant and familiar network of feeling.

The emigrants took what they could in belongings, money, and mementoes. According to one tradition, a handful of native soil wrapped in a cloth was taken along—to be buried with them eventually in alien soil. Whether or not an actual piece of sod ever had a place in the baggage of other than a few emigrants, they carried with them something more enduring—deep emotional ties to Ireland. Such has been the endurance of the tie that playwright and Harvard professor William Alfred could write in 1971 of his great-grandmother who came over "in 1866 or 1867":

> Of Ireland she rarely spoke, save to recall that she was often hungry there and that for her main meal she often ate cress out

of the brooks on oaten bread with a bit of lard. Although she always used to say she had no desire to return to Ireland to live, she lived out of a trunk to her dying day, and taught her children to do the same. I myself, till well on in my twenties, felt that Ireland, which I had never seen, was my true country. When, over eighty, she died in the early thirties, it did not seem strange six months afterward to receive a clipping from an Irish newspaper, which read: "Died in Exile: Anna Maria Gavin Egan." [4]

In emigrating, the Irish were torn from the fabric of the familiar. They came from their intimate social existences into the harsh, impersonal world of trans-Atlantic traffic. They became objects and, as such, targets of shippers, agents, runners, ship's crews, and ship's captains. They left Ireland in order to stop being victimized and, immediately, came face to face with a process that preyed upon them just as greedily.

Liverpool, from which most Irish emigrants sailed for America, was a lesson in their vulnerability. The port that had grown rich with five-sixths of Britain's slave trade handled two-thirds of its emigration. As a former mayor of Liverpool told an official inquiry in 1851, emigrants were victimized, cheated, and plundered at every opportunity from the time they reached Liverpool [5]—and even before.

Typically, Irish emigrants travelled by small steamboats from Cork or Dublin to Liverpool. At mid-century, they spent 22 to 36 hours on open decks, drenched by the seas, seasick from the unfamiliar rocking of the boat, covered often with their own vomit, arriving in a state of shock. As one director of a shipping line admitted, any covering that existed on the steamboats was designed for transporting Irish cattle (the original impetus in the 1820's for developing steam service between Dublin and Liverpool). The pigs carried between decks were treated better, since there was more interest in their welfare.

When the steamboats reached Liverpool, runners literally

attacked the bewildered passengers, grabbing their baggage, pulling them to shipping brokers and boarding houses. The favorite trick was to "capture" the emigrant by taking hold of his luggage; the traveller was sure to follow. One group of runners, aptly called the Forty Thieves, would not surrender the luggage until the emigrant paid an exorbitant price for their "service"; and they were big enough to enforce the price.

At mid-century, the runners were described as more powerful than the Catholic clergy and they ran rapaciously from victim to victim. They either owned or were connected with boarding houses, the next stop in fleecing emigrants by charging them high prices and crowding them into wretched quarters, often cellars, while they waited for their ships to sail. The shipping brokers, in turn, needed passengers to earn commissions or to fill ships they had chartered. So there were mercenary machinations to get passengers via runners and boarding houses. For good measure, the emigrants were charged outrageous prices for anything they bought and wherever possible their money was exchanged for American dollars at a larcenous rate (known as being "dollared"). Then, to close the circle, a gang of runners in Liverpool would write ahead to New York with full details on emigrants they had just fleeced so a New York gang would be waiting. At the height of Irish emigration, Liverpool lived up to Herman Melville's description of it—abounding "in all the variety of land-sharks, land-rats, and other vermin" who gnawed at impoverished Irish emigrants.

It could even be dangerous boarding the ship on the final step from the British Isles. Passengers had to scramble aboard, pushing, pulling, tugging, climbing over each other. Ships were boarded at the last minute, in pandemonium, as the captains often would not allow passengers on board until the cargo was stowed away. Eyewitnesses described what they saw after the human cargo loaded itself on board: men, women, and children uncertain about the voyage ahead, dazed from the

Liverpool experience, heartbroken about leaving home. They were beginning what an American reporter described in a Boston publication as "another dreary chapter of an existence made up of periods of strife with hard adversities."

What emigrants saw in the advertisements and heard in the honeyed words of shipping brokers was not what they experienced on board ship. What they found provoked John Francis Maguire to comment in the late 1860's when he wrote *The Irish in America*: "There are few sadder episodes in the history of the world than the story of the Irish Exodus." As Maguire reported, the ships described in "glowing accounts" on posters seen near the chapel gate by Irish peasants at Sunday mass "were but too often old and unseaworthy, insufficient in accommodation, without the means of maintaining the most ordinary decency, with bad or scanty provisions, not having even an adequate supply of water for a long voyage." There were even greater dangers, Maguire warned, than sickness, death, and a grave in the ocean: "There was no protection against lawless violence and brutal lust on the one hand, or physical helplessness and moral prostration on the other." [6]

Travelling to America was a nightmare during the days of sailing ships, which prevailed until the 1860's when steamships took over trans-Atlantic travel. Before 1845, the journey by sailing ship lasted from four to ten weeks or longer; one hapless journey took as long as 23 weeks. For travel, April and May were the best months, July and August the most problematic (because of the prevalence of southwest winds).

During the Famine Years, the Irish travelled to the United States from Liverpool on American packets, sailing ships that had a regular run between the same ports. Unlike the British ships, which were built for cargo, the American ships were built for passengers, tried to maintain schedules, and specialized in cheap passage in steerage. Whereas British ships went to British North America out of Dublin and Cork, American ships sailed to New York and Boston out of Liverpool. (In the 1840's, nine-tenths of the emigrants out of Liverpool were Irish Catholics and four-fifths sailed on U.S. ships.) The names of the American ships, which became famous among the Irish, had the ring of hope and Yankee Doodle—Boston-bound packets like *Washington Irving, Daniel Webster, Chariot of Fame*; New York-bound vessels like *Queen of the West, New World, Constitution, Star of the West.* A Liverpool-to-New York packet, the *Yorkshire*, was the fastest, averaging 29 days and once making the trip in 16. She was also the biggest earner in her career between 1843 and 1862, the year she was lost en route to Liverpool, presumably after striking an iceberg.

With the supply of ships rushing to keep up with demand, the Famine Years provided the dreariest and most dangerous chapter of Irish emigrant travel to America. Many a creaky ship was put into Atlantic service and some were not seaworthy at all. One ship preparing to leave from a small harbor in County Cork had rotten rigging, a leaking hull, and a steerage in shambles; another ship is reported to have sunk within sight of land and of relatives who had come to say farewell. Thus the name "coffin ships" and then "fever ships," where a form of typhus swept through the passengers.

The British, because of their ships, were once again the culprits. The traffic to British North America, dominated by British ships, produced a shocking casualty rate in the Famine Year of 1847; of almost 87,000 who departed, one out of six perished. By contrast, in the same year, New York had only one death for every 145 immigrants.

Life in steerage was miserable at best and the emigrants were at the harsh mercies of rough crews and skippers who usually ranged from indifferent to cruel. (There were exceptions, such as one Captain Luce, who went down with his ship in 1854, and was praised in his journal by Nathaniel Hawthorne, U.S. consul in Liverpool during the 1850's.) Space, food, air, and sanitary facilities were at a suffocating minimum, as shippers crammed in as large a human cargo as possible. Each berth held four adults, allotting 18 inches per person, a space six feet by six feet. Typically, two tiers of such berths were squeezed between the main deck and the hold of the ship in what was described by one observer as a "promiscuous heap" of men, women, and children.

Storms at sea added seasickness and terror to the misery of the company in steerage. One passenger recalled the tossing of the ship in a storm which made the passengers "frantic in despair. . . . their cries were loud enough to rise above the storm and reach to Heaven."

"Ah! Sir," said one desperate Irishman, "we thought we couldn't be worse off than we war; but now to our sorrow we know the differ; for sure supposin' we were dyin' of starvation, or if the sickness overtuk us. We had a chance of a doctor, and if he could do no good for our bodies, sure the priest could for our souls; and then we'd be buried along wid our people, in the ould church-yard, with the green sod over us, instead of dyin like rotten sheep thrown into a pit, and the minit the breath is out of our bodies, flung into the sea to be eaten up by them horrid sharks."

Ship masters who sailed on the "coffin ships" of the 1840's were saying that they surpassed the horror of the slave ships plying the Atlantic from Africa to America. British naval captain William Huskisson told the House of Commons that the condition of many ships he had seen arrive at Newfoundland "beggared all descriptions of the state of the captured slave ships." One public-spirited Irish landlord, Stephen E. DeVere, personally travelled in steerage to find out what it was like. This was in 1847 which the *London Times* called the "black year" of the emigration. By all accounts, his description of the trip differed more in degree than in detail from the typical experiences of large numbers of Irish emigrants in steerage on sailing ships:

> Before the emigrant has been a week at sea he is an altered man. How can it be otherwise? Hundreds of poor people, men,

women, and children of all ages, from the drivelling idiot of ninety to the babe just born, huddled together without light, without air, wallowing in filth and breathing a fetid atmosphere, sick in body, dispirited in heart, the fever patients lying between the sound, in sleeping places so narrow as almost to deny them the power of indulging, by a change of position, the natural restlessness of the disease; by their ravings disturbing those around, and predisposing them, through the effects of the imagination, to imbibe the contagion; living without food or medicine, except as administered by the hand of casual charity, dying without the voice of spiritual consolation, and buried in the deep without the rites of the Church.

The food is generally ill-selected and seldom sufficiently cooked, in consequence of the insufficiency and bad construction of the cooking places. The supply of water, hardly enough for cooking and drinking, does not allow washing. In many ships the filthy beds, teeming with all abominations, are never required to be brought on deck and aired; the narrow space between the sleeping berths and the piles of boxes is never washed or scraped, but breathes up a damp and fetid stench. . . .

The meat was of the worst quality. The supply of water shipped on board was abundant, but the quantity served out to the passengers was so scanty that they were frequently obliged to throw overboard their salt provisions and rice (a most important article of their food) because they had not water enough both for the necessary cooking and the satisfying of their raging thirst afterwards. They could only afford water for washing by withdrawing it from the cooking of their food. I have known persons to remain for days together in their dark, close berths because they thus suffered less from hunger. . . . Once or twice a week ardent spirits were sold indiscriminately to the passengers, producing scenes of unchecked blackguardism beyond description. . . .[7]

As steamships took over, travel became faster and easier on emigrants. If only by cutting the length of the trip by more than half, life in steerage below deck became less punishing. The food was more or less palatable, thanks to the cooking facilities available from steam, and the sanitary conditions far better. The shift from sail that gained momentum in the 1850's meant that, after the U.S. Civil War, the large majority of Irish emigrants were travelling by steamship. By 1865, more than three-quarters of all emigrants arriving in New York came by steam.

Steerage remained the lowest form of travel—life below deck amidst crowded, crude conditions, a scene portrayed by Robert Louis Stevenson after he travelled to America in 1879. He went second cabin class, next to steerage . . . "the place is lit with two lanterns. . . . The yellow flicker of the lantern spun round and round and tossed the shadows in masses. The air was hot, but it struck a chill. . . . From all around in the dark bunks the scarcely human noises of the sick joined into a kind of farmyard chorus . . . the hateful coughing and retching, and the sobs of children." The rest of the passengers were "ladies and gentlemen," those in steerage listed as "males and females."

But the time spent in steerage was never more than an impatient prelude, a necessary rite of passage in order to get to America. The emigrant mood, as described by Thomas Colley Grattan, British consul in Boston in the 1840's, rejected the fact of oceanic separation between Ireland and America. "It is, in fact, unquestionable that the Irishman looks upon America as the refuge of his race, the home of his kindred, the heritage of his children and their children," Grattan wrote in 1859.

> The Atlantic is, to his mind, less a barrier of separation between land and land, than is St. George's Channel. The Shores of England are farther off, in his heart's geography, than those of New York or Massachusetts. Degrees of latitude are not taken into account, in the measurements of his enthusiasm. Ireland— old as she is, and fond as he is of calling her so—seems to him but a part and parcel of that great continent which it sounds, to

his notions, unnatural to designate as the *new* world. He has no feeling towards America but that of love, and loyalty. To live on her soil, to work for the public good, and die in the country's service, are genuine aspirations of the son of Erin, when he quits the place of his birth for that of his adoption.[8]

III

"From the Frying Pan Into the Fire"

FOR IRISH COUNTRY PEOPLE fleeing the Famine, the trans-Atlantic trip carried them from the toils of Liverpool to the perils of New York and Boston. Their welcoming party was a mob of runners, more ruthless American counterparts of the "vermin" of Liverpool; their initial hosts were typically money-sucking rooming-house keepers; their exploiters, as in the old country, were agents of landlords. Their pride as well as their purse was under attack as anti-Irish epithets and bigotry were added to exploitation. One observer noted that the landlord's agent still victimized them, this time in milking money from tenement dwellers. He described their plight in terms of "the homely adage—'from the frying pan into the fire.'"

Like other massive waves of immigrants, the Irish were caught up in a life of continuous crisis and challenge. The peasant who left behind the harshness of his homeland faced the cruelties of a new country which dared him to thrive. The ferry ride to Liverpool, the experience there, and the suffocating, seasick life in steerage were only a prelude to the lifelong effort to sink new roots in American cities. Sources of Irish-American pugnacity are obvious right from the time of their arrival and early adjustment. Fighting back was part of surviving and Americanizing.

During the peak years of their arrival, the Irish confronted runners who jumped on board ship "in the style of plunderers or pirates." A typical scene, as described by a contemporary account, erupted in swearing, pushing, shoving, and general tumult "as great as ever was heard at Babel." In this particular example, 300 to 400 runners boarded a single ship, grabbed luggage and immigrants and tried to drag them to their favored rooming houses—besides extorting outrageous charges for carrying baggage. In appearance, the runners were "as disgusting as their horrid oaths"—"without coats, without cravats, with shirt necks flying open, a large roll of tobacco in each cheek, the juice from which, exuding down the corners of their mouths, adds to the unsightliness of their cadaverous aspect." Besides being paid for luring new arrivals to rooming houses and grog shops and selling tickets (sometimes forged) for inland travel, the runners had a caper which they called "Playing at Trunk Loo"—stealing trunks from passengers. On that day, they made off with almost 39 trunks, some of them containing all the money their newly-arrived owners had.[1]

Critics of the plundering activities of runners were loud in their condemnation. "It would literally require volumes to recount the nefarious doings of these prowling harpies," wrote one observer. "A runner is a man who is desirous of assisting you with your baggage, who professes to know a great deal, and who advises you to go to a particular hotel, eating-place or boarding-house with which he is connected. In reality he belongs to a class of tormentors, cheats and money-suckers—as annoying and far more dangerous than if you were threatened with an attack by a wolf, offered up to the stings of a hive of wasps, or seduced into the folds of a rattlesnake." The *New York Tribune* described a runner as a brute whom fire would not burn, rope hang nor water drown, whose fist was like a sledgehammer and whose strength was greater than a bull's.

The Irish had their own kind to blame, as well as native Americans. The road to exploitation was paved with false, green-tinted camaraderie or outright bullying by Irish runners. Immigrants were already being warned in the early nineteenth century about con men filled with blarney. Clements Burleigh, who lived in the United States for 30 years, wrote a letter of advice alerting immigrants to the "crowd of poor Irish" who met incoming shiploads of immigrants. They befriended new arrivals and encouraged them to visit a grog shop. "The feelings of the open-hearted Irishman are alive to the invitation, and some days are spent in this way, in the company of men who are a disgrace to the country they came from, and who are utterly incapable to procure themselves work, much less the poor emigrant," he wrote. "I warn emigrants, therefore, to be upon their guard." [2]

For the thousands arriving yearly in steerage the ordeal became an American trauma that symbolized the hard road ahead. Each remembered his or her own experience, particularly the pitfalls. A red-headed, six-foot Irishman who landed in New York in 1848 "to better his fortune," years later recalled, in conversation with Irish observer and journalist John Francis Maguire, the day he arrived with "a box of tools, a bundle of clothes and a few pounds in gold." One runner grabbed the tools, another the clothing; the runners, who wore the same uniform of loud green necktie and heavy brogue, wanted to take him to two different boarding houses. Figuring the tools were more valuable than the clothes, he followed them to a boarding house where the proprietor announced that he was from "the ould counthry, and loved every sod of it, God bless it!"

The proprietor also warned him to stay off New York's perilous streets and offered the house's food and drink—at a charge of course. Upon hearing that the young man wanted to get to Canal Street where a friend was waiting with a job, the proprietor advised him: "Canal Street!—is it Canal Street— why then what a mortal pity, and the stage to go just an hour before you entered this very door! My, my! that's unfortunate isn't it? Well, no matter, there'll be another in two days' time, or three at farthest, and I'll be sure to see you sent there all right—depend your life on me when I say it."

So for two days, the red-headed newcomer and a companion remained holed up in the rooming house until curiosity overcame timidity. They went out and roamed the streets. Finding a policeman and fellow Irishman, they asked for Canal Street. It turned out to be only a 20-minute walk to the waiting friend who, once located, went back to the rooming house and helped them retrieve their belongings. Meanwhile, according to the account, they had paid the rooming-house operator "more than would have enabled them to fare sumptuously at the Astor," then New York's most luxurious hotel.[3]

Of course, arriving in New York or Boston—or the two lesser ports of entry, Baltimore and New Orleans—was different if you were not in steerage. The maternal grandparents of the first Irish-Catholic to run for President, Alfred E. Smith, came over in 1841 with an infant son on a clipper ship of the Black Ball line, and breezed through the arrival process. They were Thomas and Maria Mulvehill from Westmeath, and Maria was the daughter of a barrister. After their ship docked at the foot of New York's Beekman Street, they walked three blocks to the corner of Dover and Water Streets, where they saw a sign: ROOMS TO LET. "They took up their abode on the second floor of a building, the ground and first floors of which were occupied by one of the old-fashioned grocery stores, owned by a German family named Dammerman," Al Smith reported. "My mother was born in that house and so was the daughter of the Dammerman family. The girls were about the same age and their friendship lasted through the years." [4]

In general, ships' captains treated their steerage passengers as they did any other cargo—to be unloaded as soon as possible. The only obstacle was the required inspection by a doctor who placed ships in thirty days' quarantine if they were dangerous to the city's health. Since this prospect appealed to neither the captain nor the passengers, steerage passengers had to scrub down their quarters on the eve of arrival, while the captain did his best to hide the lame, the halt, and the diseased. Actually, the overworked medical inspectors could not really examine anyone thoroughly. They could only look around and try to spot obvious signs of sickness.

Once past quarantine, the ships unloaded their passengers either by sending them ashore on light boats or by going directly into dock. Then it was up to the arrivals, their luck, their friends, and their personal resources to face the pitfalls. In New York, where the great majority of Irish immigrants landed, they found a city of new splendor and old squalor. Pigs roamed the streets and violence was common, while the elegant could dine at Delmonico's or buy a Titian or a Rubens on Broadway. Besides London and Paris, the other great city in the Western world was New York, whose population was being inflated by economic success and immigration—doubling to 630,000 between 1840 and 1855.

As many as 30 or 40 ships carrying immigrants might arrive in New York on a single day and the din of their arrival could be heard all over lower Manhattan. The influx was much more than the city could properly handle, particularly a haphazardly-run city like New York. Reluctant, reserved Boston, only one-third the size of New York, was hardest hit by immigration. Whereas only 5,500 immigrants had arrived in the nine years prior to 1845, 37,000 arrived in the single year 1847. In the mid-1850's, Massachusetts Governor Henry J. Gardner was reflecting the shock and mistrust of native Bostonians when he spoke before his Legislature of the need to "regulate" the newcomers. Whatever the rhetoric or the port of entry, the Irish flowed in with the tide, were tossed up on the shore, and left to their own devices.

Cautiously feeling their way in a strange land, the immigrants had to beware at every step. They were regarded as fair game and were victimized wherever they turned—to exchange money, buy some milk, a coat, a ticket for a canal boat. There were also "hundreds of pickpockets" prowling the piers, as recorded by a mid-century diarist. Robert Louis Stevenson noted in 1879 that he was "at first amused, and then somewhat staggered, by the cautious and grisly tales that went the round" as his ship approached New York's harbor.

Positive action was taken in at least one direction by New York officials, when Castle Garden at the tip of Manhattan was converted into a supervised landing depot—with runners excluded. A 13-foot wall was built around what had once been a fort and, beginning August 1, 1855, all immigrants were brought there directly from their ships. Castle Garden was a circular auditorium (billed as the largest in the world) which could hold 6,000 to 15,000 persons. As a center for entertainment and public meetings, it had housed circuses and menageries and was home for Jenny Lind's concerts. For immigrants, it became a haven from sharks, con men, and runners (the latter went to court to claim loss of rights, held protest meetings, and even shot off rockets over Castle Garden—but they lost).

Until 1892 when Ellis Island became the port of entry, immigrants moved through Castle Garden, where their luggage was protected, honest rates of exchange given for their money, properly-priced rail tickets sold, reputable boarding houses and hotels listed. At times as many as 2,000 people slept on the floor of Castle Garden, saving their funds while waiting to move on. There they had wash rooms, free hot water, and milk, bread, cheese, sausages, tea, and coffee at low prices.

Officials took in hand children sent alone to join relatives and "with a label fastened around their bodies showing their destination, forwarded them like express parcels."

Already, other labels were being tacked onto the Irishman, sometimes as a figure of fun, at other times of fear. The stage Irishman was played for laughs, done up in tattered rags, thick brogue, and heavy-handed absurdities. He boasted, waved a shillelagh and, when he spoke, out came *begorra* and *Erin go bragh*. Newspapers set the newcomers apart in stories that referred to "an Irishman" or "a foreigner." As an Irish schoolmaster in New York, Patrick S. Casserly, complained in 1832, "If a swindler, thief, robber, or murderer, no matter what his color or country, commit any nefarious or abominable act, throughout the Union, he is instantly set down as a native of Ireland."

George Potter cites a widely-circulated description of the Irish which indicted them by religious aspersions, by comparison with other groups, and by temperament. The brief, bigoted bill of indictment summarized the attitudes which the Irish had to overcome in the process of Americanization:

> The children of bigoted Catholic Ireland, like the frogs which were sent out as a plague against Pharaoh, have come into our homes, bed-chambers, and ovens and kneading troughs. Unlike the Swedes, the Germans, the Scots, and the English, the Irish when they arrive among us, too idle and vicious to clear and cultivate land, and earn a comfortable home, dump themselves down in our large villages and towns, crowding the meaner sort of tenements and filling them with wretchedness and disease. In a political point of view, what are they but mere marketable cattle.[5]

The Irish were already tarred by the British image of them, as Samuel Griswold Goodrich noted in the 1840's while warning his fellow Americans of the "spell" cast by British books, papers, and pamphlets. They try, he said, to "vindicate the tyranny of the government in Ireland, by portraying the Irish as an untamable race, deaf to reason, and only to be ruled by the harsh inflictions of power. Let us, Americans, see that our minds are not driven from the moorings of justice, by this sinister current in which they are placed."

The newly-arrived Irish were making New York their Dublin; indeed a city which would eventually have more Irish inhabitants than Dublin. In 1820, New York City had 25,000 Catholics, most of them Irish; by 1850, it was already one-third Irish (counting the 26 percent who were foreign-born Irish and their offspring in a city of a half-million). Brooklyn, then a separate city, was also gathering in the Irish. Taken together, Brooklyn and New York were more than one-third Irish by the closing decades of the nineteenth century. By 1845, one out of five Bostonians was Irish; a jump from one in 50 ten years earlier; by the end of the nineteenth century half of Boston was Irish.

The pattern became clear as Irish immigration mounted: they were country folk who were becoming city people. A nineteenth-century English observer, Philip H. Bagenal, in describing the way in which the Irish settled right where they landed, said they had "blocked up the channels of immigration at the entrance, and remain like the sand which lies at the bar of a river mouth." Bagenal depicted the "descendants of the great Irish exodus of 1845–1848" as "tired migratory birds" that had fallen on America's eastern shores.[6]

After landing in New York and Boston, the Irish were thrust into the depths of tenement squalor. Even official accounts became overheated in describing their living conditions. A committee named by the New York State Assembly to investigate housing in New York and Brooklyn reported in 1857 that its members "have witnessed, in their explorations, much calculated to shock the sensibilities and pain the heart. They have looked upon poverty in its nakedness, vice in its depravity." Depicting the "condition of a great bulk of the foreigners daily landed at our wharves," the report found "these poor strangers, these immigrants . . . destitute, dispirited, sick, ignorant, abject."

The "most important phases" of the immigrant plight, reported the committee, "must be sought in crowded shanties and tenant-houses where newly-arrived ship-loads are quartered upon already domiciled 'cousins,' to share their 'bit and sup,' until such time as 'luck' may turn up or the entire colony go to the poor-house, or be carried off by fever or smallpox."

The committee inspected "hundreds of dilapidated, dirty and densely populated old structures" which had been euphemistically labeled as renovated. In noting that the Irish predominated as occupants of such buildings, the committee members added that "in some of the better class of houses built for tenantry, negroes have been preferred as occupants to Irish or German poor; the incentive of possessing comparatively decent quarters appearing to inspire the colored residents with more desire for personal cleanliness and regard for property than is impressed upon the whites of their own condition. . . ." [7]

The commissioners of the Metropolitan Board of Health summed up the "insalubrious condition of most of the tenement houses" in New York and Brooklyn: "These houses are generally without any reference to the health or comfort of the occupant, but simply with a view to economy and profit to the owner. The provision for ventilation and light is very insufficient, and the arrangements of water-closets or privies could hardly be worse if actually intended to produce disease. These houses were almost invariably crowded, and ill-ventilated to such a degree as to render the air within them continually impure and offensive. . . ." [8]

Here are New York tenement scenes from various official reports in the mid-nineteenth century:[9]

Passing from apartment to apartment, until we reached the upper garret, we found every place crowded with occupants, one room only 5½ by 9 feet, and a low ceiling, containing two adults and a daughter of twelve years, and the father working as a shoemaker in the room, while in the upper garret were found a couple of dark rooms kept by haggard crones, who nightly supplied lodgings to twenty or thirty vagabonds and homeless persons. This wretched hiding-place of men, women, and girls who, in such places become daily more vicious and more wretched, had long been a hot-bed of typhus, seven of the lodgers having been sent to the fever hospital, while permanent residents on the lower floors had become infected with the same malady and died.

Through a narrow alley we enter a small courtyard which the lofty buildings in front keep in almost perpetual shade. Entering it from the street on a sunny day, the atmosphere seems like that of a well. . . .

Making our way through the enclosure, and descending four or five steps, we find ourselves in the basement of the rear-building. We enter a room whose ceiling is blackened with smoke, and its walls discoloured with damp. In front, opening on a narrow area covered with green mould, two small windows, their tops scarcely level with the courtyard, afford at noonday a twilight illumination to the apartment. Through their broken frames they admit a damp air laden with effluvia which constitutes the vital atmosphere imbibed by all who are immured in this dismal abode.

A door at the back of this room communicates with another which is entirely dark, and has but one opening. Both rooms together have an area of about 18 feet square, and these apartments are the home of six persons. The father of the family, a day labourer, is absent; the mother, a wrinkled crone at thirty, sits rocking in her arms an infant, whose pasty and pallid features tell that decay and death are usurping the place of health and life. Two older children are in the street. . . . A fourth child, emaciated to a skeleton, and with that ghastly and unearthly look which marasmus impresses on its victims, has reared its feeble frame on a rickety chair against the window sill, and is striving to get a glimpse at the smiling heavens whose light is so seldom permitted to gladden its longing eyes. Its youth has battled nobly against the terribly morbid and devitalizing agents which have depressed its childish life—the poisonous air, the darkness, and the damp; but the battle is nearly over, it is easy to decide where the victory will be.

During the early 1880's, when Philip Bagenal visited Irish tenements, he reacted with rage at the atmosphere "of degradation and human demoralization." Inspection "of these human rookeries" left him with "a vehement desire to pull down and raze to the ground the vast system which holds in bondage thousands and thousands of men, women, and children." [10]

Boston was just as oppressive. An 1849 committee investigating an outbreak of cholera cited "the very wretched, dirty and unhealthy condition" of houses occupied by Irish immigrants. Entire families of several persons, sometimes two or more families, were crowded into a single room amidst filth and fetid air. One district was described as "a perfect hive of human beings, without comforts and mostly without common necessaries; in many cases, huddled together like brutes, without regard to sex, or age or sense of decency; grown men and women sleeping together in the same apartment, and sometimes wife and husband, brothers and sisters, in the same bed." Such houses commonly had only one sink for everyone and one privy—"usually a mass of pollution"—for as many as 100 persons. Warehouses and factories, as well as single-family homes, were converted into dreary dwelling units. So were cellars that were entirely below ground, receiving their only air and daylight through the doorway. Landlords not only stuffed families into such cellars, but also added a grocery and vegetable shop, even a groggery and dancing hall. The committee pointed an accusing finger at genteel Boston: "How long the lamp of life, under such circumstances, holds out to burn, even for a day, is, perhaps, as great a wonder as that such a state of things should, in this community, be suffered to exist." [11]

Greedy middle men profited. The Boston committee noted that such exploiters leased entire buildings, then parceled them out, enforcing prompt payment of rent "under the threat, always rigidly executed, of immediate ejection." A report on sanitary conditions in New York described the way in which wealthy landlords could wash their hands of the conditions. The buildings were farmed out to the middle men who paid the owners what was considered a fair return on their investment. Then the middle men were free to reap large profits on the additional rents they could "extort from the wretched tenants. . . ." "[They] contrive to absorb most of the scanty surplus which remains to the tenants after paying for their miserable food, shelter, and raiment." The investigators called the situation "a state of abject dependence and vassalage little short of actual slavery."

Of such a state of affairs, John Francis Maguire, who came to visit his countrymen in the United States after the Civil War, commented bitterly: "The poor Irishman who leaves his own country to escape from the tyranny of the most grinding landlord, and becomes the slavish vassal of one of these blood-suckers, makes but a poor exchange. The 'improvement' in his condition might be fittingly indicated by the homely adage—'from the frying pan into the fire.'"

The tenements were prisons for the poor that imposed demoralization and disease. Eventually, the Irish—as did other immigrant groups—broke out of this vicious circle, but at a heavy price in human suffering. The statistics summed up the Irish poverty and individual scenes illustrated them. One prominent Irishman told the visiting Maguire that he could never forget the sight "of a miserable old Irish woman who, as the snow lay on the ground, and a bitter wind swept through the streets, was begging one Sunday morning on Broadway. Her hair was almost white, her look that of starvation, and the clothing, if such it could be called, as scanty as the barest decency might permit. Shivering and hungry, she held out her lean hands in mute petition to well-clad passers-by—her air and attitude as much a prayer for compassion in God's name, as if her tongue had expressed it in words." [12]

In his study of Boston's immigrants, Harvard historian Handlin has called pauperism "the most important and the most pervasive" of Irish misfortunes in America.[13] In New York, when the Irish constituted 25 percent of the city's 600,000 people, they filled almost 70 percent of the relief rolls. In 1876, when hard times hit New York City, it was estimated that, for every four Irishmen, there was one pauper—compared to a ratio of one for every 21 Germans (as the largest immigrant group with which they overlapped, the Irish were constantly being compared unfavorably with the Germans).

It was the poverty, of course, that drove the Irish into urban hovels, and their living conditions, in turn, bred sickness and early death. One comparison of German and Irish infant mortality for a three-month period of 1877 found that 80 percent of the babies born to Irish fathers in New York died, compared with 35 percent of those born to German fathers. Across the spectrum of deadly diseases, the Irish share was consistently higher than their share of population. A study of insurance figures showed in 1875 that Irish life expectancy was "very considerably less" than that of native Americans. In Boston, the Irish lived an average of only 14 years after arriving. The particular killers of the Irish were bronchitis, consumption, cancer, diarrhoeal diseases, and Bright's disease of the kidneys (linked to alcoholism).

An anonymous Irish mother summed up the Irish plight when an inspector from New York's health department visited her dank room in a rear courtyard. Finding her tipsy, he asked why she drank. She answered: "If you lived in this place, you would ask for whisky instead of milk." [14]

IV

Water Power, Steam Power, and "Irish Power"

FOR ALL THEIR POVERTY, Irish immigrants brought a rich resource to America—the manpower that the New World needed in order to grow and prosper. In pointing out that Ireland supplied "the most part" of the "inexhaustible fund" of energy needed for the development of America, one newspaper aptly commented: "There are several sorts of power working at the fabric of this Republic—water power, steam power and Irish power. The last works hardest of all."

The Irish were needed to dig, build, clean, chop, haul, sweep, and sweat. They came to a land where the native population shunned back-breaking jobs, and the Irish were willing, able, and faced with no other choice. For the most part, the Irish arrived with little money and no skills. What they had to offer was physical strength and a need to get to work as soon as possible. Typically, they arrived with enough money to last a week or two and immediately went in search of some kind of job.

An Irish priest writing in the *Boston Pilot* bemoaned their escape from the "emaciating poorhouse" of Ireland "with barely the passage money," so that on arrival the immigrants "must have recourse to their only means of subsistence— namely, street or yard laborers or house servants."[1] Newly- arrived Irishmen were hired as carters, porters, waiters, street cleaners, livery stable hands, bartenders, hod carriers, steve- dores, longshoremen and construction workers. For their labors, they were called greenhorns, clodhoppers, cattle Irish, Harps, Micks, blacklegs. The women, who supplied domestic help, were called biddies, pot wallopers, kitchen canaries, Bridgets.

The Irish were literally building the cities into which they crowded as America became an urban society. In 1830, only 10 percent of the U.S. population lived in cities; by the end of the century, the figure had risen to 40 percent. That meant labor was needed to build houses, streets, and water, sewer and subway systems.

They also provided the labor for an expanding country as canals were dug and railroads built into the nation's nerve system. As the flamboyant Irish-American journalist, Thomas D'Arcy McGee, proclaimed, Ireland supplied "the hands which led Lake Erie downwards to the sea, and wedded the strong Chesapeake to the gentle Delaware, and carried the roads of the East out to the farthest outpost of the West." In reviewing "Forty Years of American Life," Dr. Thomas L. Nichols, a native of New Hampshire who eventually went to live in London, noted in 1864: "The Irish in America have been a source of wealth and strength. One can hardly see how the heavy work of the country could have been done without them."

An analysis of Boston's work force in 1850 documents the

concentration of newly-arrived Irish in hard labor and domestic work. Almost half of the Irish working population were laborers and another 15 percent were domestic servants. No other group in Boston was so limited in the jobs they filled, not even black Bostonians (of whom only one-fifth were laborers). No other group depended so much upon unskilled work.[2]

In his 1882 account of Irish-Americans, Bagenal found half of New York City's Irish "engaged at common drudgery of the severest and worst-paid kind"—compared with one-fifth of native Americans and one-sixth of German-Americans. On the basis of such statistics, Bagenal noted that "in New York we find the Irish dying faster than any others, and more given to hard work and fasting than any others." [3]

The Irish were viewed by upper-class Americans "as almost as remote from us in temperament and constitution as the Chinese." As sinews of the city they were invisible, lifting native Americans to prosperity. Only something unusual brought them to attention, such as "a strange, weird, painful scene" witnessed on July 7, 1857, by George Templeton Strong, a prominent lawyer who was one of New York City's two great nineteenth-century diarists. The scene, which prompted his allusion to the Irish as being as alien as the Chinese, occurred at excavations for new houses on Fourth Avenue. A crowd had gathered after two Irish laborers had been crushed by a cave-in. Dragged out, lifeless, they lay "white and stark on the ground where they had been working, ten or twelve feet below the level of the street." They were surrounded by a few men and 15 or 20 Irish women who had clambered down.

The women were "raising a wild, unearthly cry, half shriek and half song, wailing as a score of daylight Banshees, clapping their hands and gesticulating passionately. Now and then one of them would throw herself down on one of the corpses, or wipe some trace of defilement from the face of the dead man with her apron, slowly and carefully, and then resume her lament. It was an uncanny sound to hear, quite new to me. Beethoven would have interpreted it into music worse than the allegretto of the *Seventh Symphony*." [4]

Ireland, and then Boston and New York, were used as recruiting centers for Irish laborers to work on the canals—the Erie, the Champlain, the Chesapeake, and Ohio—and on the railroads. In Ireland, the advertisements offered dazzling blandishments to men in the depths of poverty—"meat three times a day, plenty of bread and vegetables, with a reasonable allowance of liquor, and eight, ten, or twelve dollars a month for wages."

What the Irish found in the ruthless economic atmosphere of nineteenth-century America was the opportunity to be devoured by the work, the death rate, and the exploitation. Labor contractors misled them at handsome profits; subcontractors in remote construction camps charged scandalous prices for supplies; builders contrived to keep wages down by recruiting more laborers than they needed.

Desperation drove the Irish to such jobs, and so many died that, when the railroads were built, it was said there was "an Irishman buried under every tie." Irishmen were recruited for the Erie Railroad, the Illinois Central, the Western and Atlantic Railroad, the Union Pacific. They sang in bitter rhymes of what happened to them when they came over to work on the railroads:

> In eighteen hundred and forty-two
> I left the Old World for the New.
> Bad cess to the luck that brought me through
> To work upon the railway.
>
> In eighteen hundred and forty-three
> 'Twas then that I met sweet Molly McGee.
> An elegant wife she's been to me
> While working on the railway.

In eighteen hundred and forty-four
I traveled the land from shore to shore,
I traveled the land from shore to shore
To work upon the railway.

In eighteen hundred and forty-five
I found myself more dead than alive.
I found myself more dead than alive
From working on the railway

It's "Pat do this" and "Pat do that,"
Without a stocking or cravat,
Nothing but an old straw hat
While I worked on the railway.

In eighteen hundred and forty-seven
Sweet Biddy McGee she went to heaven;
If she left one kid she left eleven,
To work upon the railway.

In the South, where New Orleans served as the labor depot,
Irish laboring gangs were a standard feature of pre-Civil War
life. Page after page of municipal records listed names of
Irishmen paid $1.25 a day to build streets, levees, wharves, and
bridges over canals. They also built the canals at a high cost in
lives—as many as 20,000 in the case of a new canal cited in a
limerick published by the New Orleans *Times Picayune* on
July 18, 1837:

Ten thousand Micks, they swung their picks,
To dig the New Canal
But the choleray was stronger 'n they,
An' twice it killed them awl.

Official reports had a different rhyme; they viewed the Irish
as a social problem. The *Seventeenth Annual Report* of the
New York Association for Improving the Condition of the Poor
(1860) said that "unfortunately, they [the Irish] are mostly

rude, uninstructed laborers of the lowest grade, who have but little knowledge of work beyond what has been derived from farming their impoverished potato patch, which has given them a decided distaste for agriculture, to which they were pertinaciously attached in their own country. Hence, they are seldom found felling the forests, or turning up the virgin prairie on their own account, or, indeed, their own masters anywhere; but generally on the line of our public works, in villages, and especially in the worst portions of our large cities, where they compete with the negroes between whom and themselves there is an inveterate dislike, for the most degrading employments. With many good qualities and excellent traits of character, they are excitable and impulsive—have little thrift, economy, or forecast, and are often addicted to intemperance. It is not surprising, therefore, that so many soon find themselves at the foot of the social ladder. . . ." [5]

As a visitor to America quickly discovered, newly-arrived Irishmen were regarded as suitable for manual labor and little else. In the diary of his American tour, published in 1886, the Rev. M. B. Buckley put it bluntly: "the Yankees hate" the Irish. "Where headwork is necessary, they will not employ an Irishman, if they can help it; but where they want labour they will engage Paddy as they would a dray horse." [6] As early as 1830, the despised words, *No Blacks or Irish Need Apply*, were added to a job advertisement in the *New York Courier and Enquirer*.

Irish women, in the desperation of poverty and in the absence of skills, sought the female version of manual labor— domestic service. The advertisements of the 1830's demonstrate the bigotry facing them:

> Wanted—A Cook or a Chambermaid. They must be American, Scotch, Swiss, or Africans—no Irish —*New York Evening Post*, September 4, 1830.

Wanted—A woman well qualified to take charge of the cooking and washing of a family—any one but a Catholic who can come well recommended, may call at 57 John Street —*Journal of Commerce*, July 8, 1830.

Wanted—An English or American woman, that understands cooking, and to assist in the work generally if wished; also a girl to do chamberwork. None need apply without a recommendation from their last place. IRISH PEOPLE need not apply, nor any one that will not rise at 6 o'clock, as the work is light and the wages sure. Inquire at 359 Broadway. —*Truth Teller*, December 28, 1833, quoting the *American*.

Woman wanted—To do general housework . . . English, Scotch, Welsh, German, or any country or color except Irish. —*Daily Sun*, May 11, 1853.

By the mid-nineteenth century, however, necessity overcame prejudice. There was a severe shortage of domestic help, particularly in New England, as native Americans disdained such work. As a visitor noted during an 1857–1858 tour of America, a native American "scorns to be considered a 'servant', and if forced to work in a shop or wait on tables, such Americans regarded themselves as 'help' not as servants." The attitude was: "Let negroes be servants, and if not negroes, let Irishmen fill the place. . . ." The blacks, in turn, exhibited a dislike for the Irish, "whom they were the first to call 'white niggers.' " By the 1850's, about 80 percent of New York's foreign-born servants and waiters were Irish. Most of the remainder were Germans. Of New York Irish with jobs, a fourth were in the servant category; among Germans, only one out of ten.

In home and hotel, Irish servant girls became a fixture. They were housekeepers, nurses, chambermaids, charwomen, laundresses, and cooks. When they took care of children, their pay,

their living quarters, and their status improved. The virtues of
the Irish girl were thereby rewarded: they were hard-working,
honest, reliable, efficient, and virtuous. When asked why all
the women working in his hotel were Irish, a prominent hotel
owner summed up the reason: "The thing is very simple: the
Irish girls are industrious, willing, cheerful, and honest—they
work hard, and they are very strictly moral. I should say that is
quite reason enough." 7

While disdainful Yankees certainly would not want their
sons to marry one, they welcomed Irish servant girls into their
homes, let them run their households and raise their children.
For, in addition to all their virtues, Irish girls worked for lower
wages than native Americans. In his tour of the United States,
Maguire found Irish servant girls to be "indispensable" in
American hotels and accorded "unlimited trust" in thousands
of American homes. As to their virtue, he reported that
would-be seducers would warn their friends away from an
Irish girl—"Oh, hang her!—don't lose your time with *her;* she
is one of those d——d girls—the priest has a hold of her—she
goes to confession, and all that kind of nonsense—don't lose
your time, for it's no use."

As good Irish-Catholic girls working in the enemy camp of
Protestantism, they were tagged "Bridgets" and had to face
down condescension, if not insults. Maguire tells the story of a
live-in maid named Kate and a Protestant minister who visited
her household and regularly taunted her. At a large dinner
party one evening, Kate entered the dining room with a big
tureen of steaming soup. "Ho, ho, Bridget," jibed the minister.
"How are you, Bridget? Well, Bridget, what did you pay
Father Pat for absolution this time? Come to me, Bridget, and
I will give you as many dollars as will set you straight with the
old fellow for the next six months, and settle your account with
purgatory, too. Now, Bridget, tell us how many cents for each
sin."

It was his turn for soup as Kate served the guests, and her

turn to answer: "Now, sir, I often asked you to leave me alone, and not mind me, and not to insult me or my religion, what no real gentleman would do to a poor girl; and now, sir, as you want to know what I pay for absolution, here's my answer!"

She then poured the soup all over him. Rushing to her bedroom, she locked the door, and had a good cry. In the happy ending to the story, her mistress came to get her, saying all was well. Kate won the sympathy of all and the silence of the minister henceforth. It was also reported that Kate commented in retelling the story that the dousing did the minister "a power of good." Whether or not the story was embroidered, it did reflect what one Irish newspaper called the tendency for Irish servant girls to mistake "forwardness if not impertinence" for independence. For in general, while the Irish served, they were definitely not subservient. In fact, one observer claimed in 1870 that "terror of the Irish servant, at least as much as anything else" drove Americans into living in hotels, for "stories are told without end of the formidable revenges taken, where Irish servants have felt themselves slighted." 8

However, as unskilled labor of one kind or another, the Irish were still not masters of their economic lot. Those who had once depended on pitiful plots of land in Ireland, depended in America on a pitiless, free-enterprise economy and its ups and downs. They still depended on others for their bread and for their liquor.

As the Irish numbers mounted, two major efforts were made to improve their condition. One was to get them to leave the cities. The other was to get them to give up drinking. Neither succeeded in changing the Irish habit or habitat.

In the midst of mass migration, the voice of Irish teetotalism, Father Theobald Mathew, arrived in New York. In Ireland, the dedicated Capuchin friar claimed that he had administered the pledge to half of Ireland (exceptions made for medicinal drinking). His success, though short-lived, was dramatic: production of whisky in Ireland fell by one-half in the decade before the Famine Years. In Ireland, he linked politics to abstinence with his slogan, "Ireland sober is Ireland free" and for Irish-Americans he linked sobriety to success. During a two-year tour of the United States, he covered 37,000 miles and collected an estimated half-million pledges.

On departing in December, 1851, Father Mathew advised his transplanted countrymen that "no impediment (save of your own creation) exists to prevent your attaining the highest social and civic distinction." Therefore, he pleaded: "I implore you, as I would with my dying breath, to discard forever those foolish divisions—those insensate quarrels—those factious broils (too often, alas! the fruits of intemperance) in which your country is disgraced, the peace and order of society violated, and the laws of heaven trampled on and outraged." [9]

After Father Mathew left, funds were still collected to further his efforts. The *Boston Pilot*, a newspaper of great influence among Irish-Americans, ran items listing donors, with the notice, "If any other parties feel disposed to send a little 'aid and comfort' to the good father, we shall be pleased to forward it to him." In donations for the "Apostle of Temperance," the *Pilot* listed $36 on August 26, 1854: $10 each from Arthur McAvey, Patrick B. Donahoe, and Donovan, O'Connor & Co., N.Y.; $5 from Joseph B. Kelly of Boston; and $1 from James Myban, Moravia, N.Y.

The same issue of the *Boston Pilot* described the shocking effect of alcohol on some Irish wakes, one in particular that came to their attention: "A man is taken sick with the cholera. He dies without the sacraments, because he lives in the society of drunkards, who are thinking about the wake. The clergyman finds in the room a dead body, a quantity of tobacco and bad rum, and a crowd of people drinking and smoking as they would in a common bar room. Any clergyman could describe scenes of this sort which he has witnessed that would chill one's blood. Thanks be to God, these scenes are comparatively rare. But, if there were but one in the course of a year, there would be one too many."

The *Pilot* also cited "a disgraceful scene" of "far too frequent occurrence in our city"—"A number of hacks, *returning from a funeral*, were driven at furious neck-breaking speed down the street, the drivers apparently well 'corned,' and the insiders ditto, and singing, or screaming at the top of their lungs. Such practices are outrageous under any circumstances, but perpetrated by those returning from the burial of the dead, are execrable." The *Pilot* added that the hack drivers even race to the grave and that "the drivers and others will fight before the body is buried."

If Fathew Mathew provided the hopeful sermon of Irish temperance, a well-known comedian named Tom Flynn personified its more realistic rate of failure. In the late 1830's, after drinking heavily for years, he took the pledge and announced a temperance lecture in New York City's Chatham Theatre. Fellow tipplers stayed home and temperance ladies turned out to hear a celebrated convert's lecture on the evils of drink.

For two hours on a bare stage, old Tom held forth from a plain table which held only a water pitcher and a glass. As he depicted the drunkard's downfall, he evoked a convincing mixture of laughs and sighs from an enthralled audience. He stopped only to wet his lips by taking sips from the glass, which he refilled from time to time. The audience was being swept along as he stormed into his peroration, when suddenly, he hesitated, swayed, then collapsed. Amidst a wave of sympathy, he was carefully carried to a nearby hotel, while those remaining behind talked sadly of Tom Flynn's misfortune. The real climax of the temperance sermon came when someone sipped from the glass. Then the source of both inspiraton and collapse was discovered—Tom was guzzling Old Swan, his favorite gin.[10]

In reality, the parable of the comedian was closer to

observable Irish behavior than the Capuchin's abstemious sermon. Both friend and critic of the Irish provided a continuous commentary on their *problem*. The haughty diarist George Templeton Strong, who himself dabbled in chloroform and hashish, snorted that "it's as natural for a Hibernian to tipple as for a pig to grunt." As early as 1817, when the New York Irish Emigration Association asked Congress to set aside land to be settled by Irish immigrants, the formal petition cited the temptations of drink: "Before they can taste the fruits of happy industry, the tempter too often presents to their lips the cup that turns man to brute, and the vast energies which would have made the fields to blossom make the cities groan." An 1855 report on insanity in Massachusetts found that "unquestionably" much of the insanity among the Irish was due to intemperance, "to which the Irish seem to be peculiarly prone."

In his 1882 description of the Irish-American situation, Philip Bagenal pointed up the link between poverty and drink, noting that "as long as 50 percent of the Irish are poorly paid and ill-fed drudges, so long will they be intemperate." Recalling his service in New York from 1873 to 1876, Bishop John Lancaster Spalding of Peoria, Illinois, argued that the official descriptions of the slums "would soil a page intended for all eyes" and that "people who live in this atmosphere and amid these surroundings must drink"—"the perfectly sober would die from mere loathing of life."

Riotous public behavior by the Irish was an obvious result of drinking. The Irish-born British consul in Boston, Thomas Colley Grattan, described the low boiling point of the Irish, so easily fueled by alcohol: "The memory of their ancient feuds in the old country revived by some chance word, they rush into conflict with their fellow-countrymen, or, in the words (scarcely exaggerated) of the song, *Get Drunk, meet their friend, and for love knock him down.*" [11] Baltimore's Archbishop Martin John Spalding, who during the mid-nineteenth century defended the Irish against their critics, wrote that the Irishman's "heart is generally in the right place" and his faults are of the head rather than the heart, his vices "generally the result of intemperance, or of the sudden heat of passion."

Maguire cited drink as the cause in nine out of ten cases where the Irish got into trouble with the law. He compared the way different nationalities handled their liquor: "The American may drink from morning to night without injury to his country, without peril to his nationality; the German may snore himself into insensibility in a deluge of lager beer, without doing dishonour to Faderland; the Englishman and the Scotchman may indulge to excess—as both do indulge to excess—without compromising England or Scotland thereby; but the Irishman, more impulsive, more mercurial, more excitable, will publish his indiscretion on the highway, and will himself identify his nationality with his folly." [12]

The Irish had long before turned to alcohol in the old country where travellers had cited their drinking problem as early as the sixteenth century. Irish immigrants came from a society where male bonding was encouraged and maintained by alcohol. This came about because poverty and the shortage of land discouraged early marriage and therefore created a pressure to keep the sexes apart. The men, who stayed together in conviviality and horseplay, drank together. Teetotalers were regarded suspiciously; they may very well have been out chasing girls. Thus Irish immigrants arrived with an ethic of hard work and hard drinking.

If whiskey was cheaper than meat in Ireland, it was even cheaper in America where the Irish could earn the money to buy its relief from the back-breaking misery of their lives. Moreover, they came to a hard-drinking country, one which had shocked its own temperance advocates. As if the Irish needed further temptation, whiskey was made a part of their pay when they worked on the railroads.

As the Irish population in the cities mounted, so did grog

shops, saloons, and liquor dealers, not to mention Irish families that sold gin illegally as a sideline. Boston felt the difference immediately. In 1846, it had 850 licensed liquor dealers; in 1849 there were 1,200. A city survey in 1851 found that the great majority were Irish-operated; Boston's mayor reported in the following year that two-thirds of the grog shops were owned by the Irish. In 1854, the *New York Tribune* reported that while Catholics comprised only one-fourth of the city's inhabitants, they ran one-half to three-fourths of the saloons.

A New York visitor during the U.S. Civil War reported that Schenck and Shaughnessy represented "the plodding Teuton and the impulsive Celt, over the portals of lager-beer saloons and whisky stores, in all the leading thoroughfares, from the back slums in the vicinity of the wharves to the pave on the Broadway, where Republican 'big bugocracy' sports its jewels, silks and drapery. . . . One of the principal trading branches of business in which Irishmen are generally successful, is that of the liquor store line, a trade which the Irish and Germans may be said to divide between them." [13]

The saloon was the "poor man's club," the "Nursery of Democracy," a local political powerhouse, and a semiofficial station on the way to U.S. citizenship. (In New York, the Tammany Democratic political machine scattered citizenship applications in saloons for distribution by bartenders. The forms carried the straightforward request, "Please naturalize the bearer"—which the nearest Tammany judge readily did.) As a meeting place where the talk, the camaraderie and the brogue were familiar, the saloon was the social center of Irish areas, a place where the poor Irishman in particular could go. He could leave his crowded, wretched home, rest his weary body, and refresh his soul.

It was said that the Irish were ready "to drink upon every thing," and this attitude was expressed in one of the many Irish tales published in mid-nineteenth-century newspapers. Paddy was being lectured on drinking by his wife while watering the horse. "Now, Paddy, isn't that baste an example to ye? Don't ye see he laves off when he has enough, the craythur!" To which Pat countered: "Oh, it's very well to discourse like that, Biddy, but if there was another horse at the side of the trough to say, 'Here's to your health, me ould boy!' would he sthop till he drank the whold trough, think ye?"

The saloon was a direct transfer of the pub that played a major role in Irish country life as a social, political, and economic center. Well into the twentieth century, the American saloon carried on this tradition, as recalled by a Chicago ward politician:

> Years ago, before what was called the regular [Democratic] organization, politicians would go to the corner saloon and the saloonkeeper was the doctor, lawyer, banker—and that's where a candidate would go on Sunday to meet the people of the community. . . .
>
> Old timers, not only Irish—Italians, and all the others—would borrow money, come in for advice. The bank was at 63rd and Halsted. People wouldn't go there on the average—they'd borrow money from the saloonkeeper. The politicians would—a fellow running for office would make ten to twenty of these different spots. It was his way of campaigning.[14]

The saloon symbolized the Irish changeover to city dwellers. It was one way of humanizing the urban environment which they had adopted so completely. They hardly listened when the cry, Go West, was raised, as in 1855, when Thomas D'Arcy McGee tried unsuccessfully to organize an Irish colonization program. On one hand, McGee celebrated the role of the Irish in America with lectures before packed houses and in books popular among Irish-Americans. But he was also sensitive to the Irish shortcomings, so evident in the slums and saloons of the city.

His peak activity ended in 1857 when, disillusioned, he moved to Canada, where he played a significant part in the growth of Canadian nationalism. (In 1868, he was assassinated by an Irish fanatic after extremists labeled his Canadian career a betrayal of Ireland.) In the United States, he used rhyme as well as rhetoric and reason to lure the Irish westward:

> In the villages of New England
> Are you happy, we would know?
> Are you welcome, are you trusted?
> Are you not? Then Rise and Go!

Catholic bishops from Western states tried to attract the Irish from their city strongholds in order to improve the immigrants' moral and economic lot, and to build up their own Catholic communities. The leading voices were Archbishop John Ireland of St. Paul and Bishop Spalding of Peoria, joined by others from Iowa, Nebraska, Wisconsin, and South Dakota (Minnesota boasted of its prolific potato crop, Wisconsin of lakes and fields like Ireland's and butter that was superior). In urging the Irish to seek the rich opportunities of open lands in the West, Bishop Spalding lamented the fact that in the 1870's only eight in every 100 Irishmen were farmers. He blamed the English for creating the deep-seated Irish attitude "that the country should have been regarded and shunned by them as a yawning grave," concluding: "Of all the fatal curses with which English tyranny has blighted Ireland, this, I think, is the worst." [15] It has been noted that Irish immigrants "rejected the land for the land had rejected them."

If, in Ireland, the land had been cruel, in America, it imposed loneliness in a remote place, a discouraging prospect for the highly-sociable Irish. These were not Scandinavians who had lived in merciless cold and stubborn isolation. The Irish wanted other people around, people whom they knew and could turn toward. Their mood was summarized by an Irishman writing home from a Missouri farm in praise of economic opportunity and social equality but with desperate longing for the sociability of the old country. "I could then go to a fair or a wake, or dance. . . . I could spend the winter nights in a neighbour's house cracking jokes by the turf fire. If I had there but a sore head I could have a neighbour within every hundred yards of me that would run to see me. But here everyone can get so much land, and generally has so much, that they calls them neighbours that live two or three miles off—och! the sorra take such neighbours, that made me leave home." [16]

In the mid-nineteenth century, New York's first archbishop, John Hughes, used his enormous influence among Irish Catholics to discourage any organized schemes for westward movement. He wanted the Irish to make such decisions individually and was against organized colonization programs. As far as he was concerned, the organizers were advising their fellow Irishmen: "Go you. We stay."

On one occasion that became a celebrated incident among Irish-Americans, the imperious archbishop delivered a dramatic counter-blow to the Go West campaign. On March 26, 1857, he attended incognito a public meeting to promote Western colonization by the Irish. At the end of the main talk, he rose from his seat in the gallery and exclaimed, "Wait a moment. I have a word to say."

A voice from the audience shouted abusively, "Come on the stand, then."

"No, I shall not," he answered. "I would rather be by myself."

Whereupon, he revealed his identity and delivered an attack upon Western colonization to the stunned audience. His particular target was an 1856 convention of Catholics in Buffalo to promote a Westward movement. While Hughes and other church leaders in the cities were accused of opposing colonization for their own purposes of power and advantage— along with saloonkeepers and politicians—he felt strongly that the Irish were unfit for the frontier.

In an unpublished document in his own handwriting, Archbishop Hughes drew a pessimistic picture of the Irish as settlers. He described the "great majority" as entirely unfit for the "multifarious industry which a settlement on wild land presupposes." The Irish immigrants, he said, did not know how to use an axe, hew and shape logs, or guide a plough, and even if they did, they lacked the money to go West and support themselves "until the combined fruitfulness of the earth and their own labor should furnish them with the sustenance of life." [17]

Bishop Spalding, expressing a widely-held view, called Archbishop Hughes' opposition "most unfortunate." "No other man has ever had such influence over the Irish Catholics of the United States," Spalding wrote, "and no other man could have done so much to make them realize that their interests for time and eternity required that they should make homes for themselves on the land." [18]

The Irish who did become farmers were as successful as any other immigrant group, though they had a tendency to develop a farm, sell it, and start another. Many Irish farmers were drawn from those men who had gone out to work on canals and railroads and remained to settle the land. Some were attracted to the goldfields of California after 1849, with Maguire reporting in the 1860's that "there is not a State in the Union in which the Irish have taken deeper and stronger root, or thriven more successfully, than California." [19] Among Far Western cities, San Francisco had the largest number of immigrants, and by 1880 the Irish were one-tenth of their number.

As to going South, Bishop John England of Charleston warned in 1840 that the "southern states are the worst places to which an Irishman can emigrate, except he is a merchant with good capital, a mechanic in the way of building or tailoring (with as much spare means as would support him for a couple of months), steady habits and untiring industry." In general, the Irish population remained limited in the South, with the largest settlement in New Orleans, where many lived in a riverfront section dubbed the "Irish Channel."

Wherever they settled, the Irish concentrated in the cities. This was documented in the 1860 U.S. Census figures on the states with the greatest number of Irish: New York, Pennsylvania, Massachusetts, Illinois, Ohio, New Jersey. (The smallest number lived in Florida, North Carolina, Oregon, Arkansas, Texas, Kansas.) Irish immigrants constituted 23 percent of New York's white population in the cities, which was twice their percentage in the rest of the state. They were one-sixth of the urban population in Pennsylvania, but only one-twenty-fifth of the rural. In Massachusetts, the Irish proportion was three times as great in Boston and twice as great in other Bay State cities when compared with rural areas; in Illinois, four times as great in Chicago as in outlying areas. The 1880 U.S. Census showed that 46 percent of all foreign-born Irish were living in only four cities: New York, Philadelphia, Brooklyn, and Boston.

Whatever happened to the Irish in America, however they felt and acted, whatever reactions they elicited, their group identity figured in. Solidarity was a source of strength and accounted for the formidable Irish role in American life, particularly in politics and religion. As newcomers huddling together, the Irish helped each other cope with the pressures of urban survival and provided themselves with the comforts of a friendly and familiar ambience. They prayed and drank together; turned out for holy days, election day, and parade day; congregated in saloons, churches, and firehouses. However, the same clear identity that gave them strength also made them targets of concerted bigotry, outright hostility, and violence. When the Irish came through the swinging doors of the New World, their noses were bloodied.

V

Adding Injury to Insult

As Irish pride confronted the prejudices of native Americans, organized bigotry and even injury were added to ordinary insult. The Irish were not only penalized in the job market. They were subjected to campaigns by nativist organizations, vilified in print and speeches, and victimized in bloody rioting.

While blarney was prominent as a weapon of self-defense in British-dominated Ireland, in America the Irish became free to deal both in bombast and in self-centered militancy. They developed a readily identifiable style that was popularly regarded as Irish pugnacity. They were castigated, in turn, for retaliating against nativist pressures and particularly criticized for "sticking together"—in where they lived (Irish ghettoes), in how they voted (Democratic), in the way they worshipped (Catholic).

The Irish had compelling reasons to stay among their own

kind. They were drawn together by misery, nostalgia, and rejection. As historian Albert Bushnell Hart of Harvard University has noted, "the Irish were thought to be too clannish, flocking by themselves and cutting themselves off from the life of the community like an alien element; although one wonders what else could have been expected in view of the attitude of mingled dislike, distrust and contempt which they so frequently encountered from the natives. In fact, they could usually find real friendliness and help only from people of 'their own kind' and from their priests." [1]

A self-perpetuating process was at work among the Irish, as with later immigrants. In sticking together, they provided a clear target for hostility. Hostility, in turn, reinforced the tendency to stick together, for it presented the Irish with an obvious choice: on one hand, acceptance amidst the protection and pleasures of their own kind; on the other hand, rejection or at least indifference among "others."

For their part, native Americans already had been sounding alarms about foreigners since the late eighteenth century. The Federalists warned of French revolutionary spies and "hordes of wild Irishmen." Nativism emerged early in the nineteenth century with the Irish as the particular target of fear and resentment. To the nativist, alien customs, habits, attitudes, and appearances threatened the American way of life. The large influx of Irish inevitably increased the resentment against them, for they constituted 43 percent of U.S. foreign-born by 1850—twice the proportion of the next largest group, the Germans.

The Irish were looked upon as out of place and out of tune with America and this created an atmosphere which readily fostered anti-Irish campaigns and rioting. Even a sympathetic observer early in the nineteenth century remarked disdainfully that the Irishman's "uncouth air, his coarse raiment, his blunders, and his brogue are unattractive or ludicrous." Two members of Parliament writing to British Prime Minister John

Russell, described the Irish as "socially despised" in America and only tolerated as a "serviceable nuisance." The letter, published in an 1847 issue of the London *Spectator*, said flatly: "If ever two nationalities came into collision by meeting, it is the Irish and the American in the United States."

The *Life and Letters of Edwin Lawrence Godkin* contain an 1859 letter from a journalist to the influential American editor, observing that it was difficult to think of "more incongruous elements" than the "jolly, reckless, good-natured, passionate, priest-ridden, whiskey-loving, thriftless Paddy, and the cold, shrewd, frugal, correct, meeting-going Yankee." Moreover, "the speculative New Englander, who has been bred in a theological atmosphere, where intellect has been sharpened ever since he learnt to speak by controversy on 'fixed fate, free will, foreknowledge,' feels little brotherhood for poor Paddy who never discussed a point of doctrine in his life." [2]

Native Americans found the Irish both funny and fearful, as well as useful. As one New Englander said in discussing the importance of the Irish working man, "We do not know what we should do without him. We do not know what we shall do with him." There were also numerous anti-Irish jokes: "What kind of a country is this?" said the Irishman trying to pick up a stone that was frozen to the ground. "You let your dogs run loose, and tie your stones."

In writing of the Irish in New Orleans, an historian has noted that "jokes and stories based on the economic and social status of the immigrants multiplied like weeds." [3] Two heavy-handed examples were printed by the New Orleans *Picayune* in 1845: "The very last Irish case we have heard, is that of a cook, who happening to let some candles fall into water, put them into the oven to dry." "When a young man seeking admission to the bar was asked to define a common carrier, he answered, 'an Irish hodman—he is the commonest kind of carrier.'" Another anecdote, reprinted in various newspapers,

concerned an Irish servant girl who was sent by the lady of the
house to get a "bed comforter" from the store and promptly
returned with one of the clerks.

To his Irish audiences, Thomas D'Arcy McGee denounced
the way the Irish were depicted in the theater: "The stage
Irishman was dressed in very old-fashioned, battered garments,
had a pipe stuck in his hat-band, held a short stick in his hand,
and cursed a little bad blasphemy. Well-dressed people—
better dressed outside than inside—applauded such extrava-
gances, and went home confident that they had seen a
veritable representation of 'the real animal.' "

Like other immigrant groups to come, the Irish were blamed
for their own miserable conditions and branded with stereo-
types. Inhabitants of squalid tenements, victims of disease and
drink, poor and uneducated, the Irish were depicted as "idle
bums and hoodlums," as "being sociable with pavin' bricks."
Diarist George Templeton Strong referred to "the lawless,
insolent arrogance and intolerance of these homicidal ruffianly
popish Celts"; to him an Irishman was a "Papistical Paddy." In
the vocabulary of nativism, Irishman and drunkard, Irishman
and hooligan were synonymous. It was noted that to be called
an "Irishman" had come to be considered almost as insulting
as to be called a "nigger." [4]

Anti-Irish rhetoric was uninhibited and a source of constant
irritation to the Irish striving for acceptance. The Chicago *Post*
of September 9, 1868, ran this portrait of "Teddy O'Flaherty":
"He has hair on his teeth. He never knew an hour in civilized
society. . . . He is a born savage—as brutal a ruffian as an
untamed Indian. . . . Breaking heads for opinion's sake is his
practice. The born criminal and pauper of the civilized world
. . . a wronged, abused, and pitiful spectacle of a man . . .
pushed straight to hell by that abomination against common
sense called the Catholic religion. . . . To compare him with
an intelligent freedman would be an insult to the latter. . . .

The Irish fill our prisons, our poor houses. . . . Scratch a convict or a pauper, and the chances are that you tickle the skin of an Irish Catholic."

In the nativist view, the words Irish and Catholic were synonymous and equally odious. This was the case even before the great immigration influx, as noted by Patrick S. Casserly, an Irish-American schoolmaster and journalistic essayist: "In this country, the idea of Catholicity and Ireland is so blended in the minds of the American people, as to be in a manner inseparable."

The same observation was made by Bishop John England, who emigrated from County Cork in 1820 and who was, at his death in 1842, the most influential U.S. Catholic prelate. After noting that it was possible to be Irish and not Catholic or Catholic and not Irish, Bishop England pointed out: "But when the great majority of the Catholics in the United States were either Irish or of Irish descent, the force of the prejudice against the Irish Catholic bore against the Catholic religion in the United States and the influence of this prejudice has been far more mysterious than is generally believed." [5]

Thus, the flourishing activity in anti-Catholic newspapers, pamphlets, and books struck at both Irish and non-Irish Catholics. The Roman Catholic Church and the papacy were labeled the Anti-Christ, the Great Red Dragon, and the Beast. A religious journal, called *The Protestant*, announced in 1829 that it intended "to inculcate Gospel doctrines against Romish corruptions" while its successor publication, the *Protestant Vindicator*, warned its readers that "it is absolutely impossible for a genuine Papist to speak the truth, or swear to the truth, if his statements will in any way injure Popery and its Priests." As early as 1835, an observer remarked that publication of anti-Catholic books "has become a part of the regular industry of the country, as much as the making of nutmegs or the construction of clocks." One Catholic historian has estimated that in 1849 alone—which he describes as a year of "comparative silence" for nativism—2.2 million pages of pamphlets attacking the Catholic Church were printed.

The most influential anti-Catholic work ever published in the United States appeared in 1836: a literary hoax titled *Awful Disclosures of Maria Monk, as exhibited in a narrative of her sufferings during a residence of five years as a Black Nun in the Hotel Dieu Nunnery in Montreal.* Upon publication in New York, the book had a ready American audience for Maria's tales of how, as a nun, she had "to live in the practice of criminal intercourse" with priests, how babies born as a result were baptized and immediately strangled, how she had taken part in midnight orgies. Actually, Maria had never been in a convent, but rather had been in an asylum for wayward girls and had run away to New York with the help of her backer, a Canadian minister noted for his rabid anti-Catholicism. Eventually her book, which was actually the work of a ghost writer, was thoroughly discredited, and Maria herself ended her days as the proverbial fallen woman. She died in a New York jail after being arrested in a house of prostitution for picking a client's pockets.

Such was the appetite for anti-Catholic literature that the book went through 20 printings and sold 300,000 copies in the period prior to the Civil War. It continued to appear in numerous editions throughout the nineteenth century, an ongoing reminder of anti-Catholicism in America. It even surfaced again in the twentieth century when two Irish Catholics ran for the Presidency, reappearing during the campaigns of Al Smith in 1928 and John Kennedy in 1960.

What some Americans wanted to believe and many others were ready to believe about the Irish and their church is reflected in excerpted samples from Maria Monk's *Awful Disclosures*:

> One of my great duties was to obey the priests in all things;
> and this I soon learnt, to my utter astonishment and horror, was

to live in the practice of criminal intercourse with them. . . . Priests, she [the Mother Superior] insisted, could not sin. It was a thing impossible. Every thing that they did, and wished, was of course right. . . .

She gave me another piece of information which excited other feelings in me, scarcely less dreadful. Infants were sometimes born in the convent: but they were always baptized and immediately strangled! This secured their everlasting happiness; for the baptism purified them from all sinfulness, and being sent out of the world before they had time to do anything wrong, they were at once admitted into heaven. How happy, she exclaimed, are those who secure immortal happiness to such little beings! Their little souls would thank those who kill their bodies, if they had it in their power! . . .

I was informed immediately after receiving the veil that infants were occasionally murdered in the Convent. I was one day in the nuns' private sick-room, when I had an opportunity, unsought for, of witnessing deeds of such a nature. Two little twin babes, the children of [Sister] Sainte Catharine, were brought to a priest, who was in the room, for baptism. . . . The priest then on duty was Father Larkin. . . . He first put oil upon the heads of the infants, as is the custom before baptism. When he had baptised the children, they were taken, one after another, by one of the old nuns, in the presence of us all. She pressed her hand upon the mouth and nose of the first, so tight that it could not breathe, and in a few minutes, when the hand was removed, it was dead. She then took the other, and treated it in the same way. No sound was heard, and both the children were corpses. The greatest indifference was shown by all present during this operation; for all, as I well knew, were long accustomed to such scenes. The little bodies were then taken into the cellar, thrown into the pit I have mentioned, and covered with a quantity of lime.

The Protestant pulpit also welcomed tales of Catholic iniquity, all the better if described by apostates (preferably, former nuns and priests). Two devoted Catholic historians—

Henry De Courcy and John Gilmary Shea—wrote with indignation in the nineteenth century of the nativist pursuit of "some apostate from Catholicity whose revelations would be racy enough to stimulate curiosity." They singled out a man named Leahy as the most celebrated of a string of impostors. A farmer's son from Templemore in Ireland, where he had worked for the Trappists, Leahy passed himself off as a former monk and for ten years had "churches and pulpits opened to him, to thunder against Catholicity and the morals of the clergy." Leahy had four wives, not to mention "the other victims of his passions" and he flourished until he appeared in court on August 20, 1852, to accuse a friend of seducing his wife. When the judge acquitted the friend, Leahy shot his rival dead in open court and wounded a lawyer who tried to stop him. Leahy ended up with a life sentence in prison (where he repented and was received back into the Catholic Church on January 20, 1856).[6]

William Cardinal O'Connell recalled the poisoned atmosphere of bigotry in which he grew up in Lowell, Massachusetts, in the 1860's. "We lived actually in an atmosphere of fear," he wrote in his autobiography. "We sensed the bitter antipathy, scarcely concealed, which nearly all these good women in charge of the schools felt toward those of us who had Catholic faith and Irish names. For any slight pretext we were severely punished. We were made to feel the slur against our faith and race, which hurt us to our very hearts' core. As all the teachers were of this same stamp, it was little wonder that from my fifth to my twelfth year school life meant nothing to me but a dreary drive, with a feeling of terror, lest, for any reason or no reason, the teacher might vent her ill feeling upon our defenseless persons."

Outside school, the future Cardinal of Boston admitted, the Irish struck back at young Yankees who jeered at them as Paddies and Biddies. "Oftentimes, contrary to the counsel of our parents and our priests," he reported, Irish boys went after their tormentors and "in time taught the much-needed lesson that young Irish-America would no longer tolerate English Puritan abuse." [7]

Another little boy who would become a power in the Irish-dominated Catholic Church was receiving his "share of insults—and rocks" in the central Indiana town of Peru. John Cardinal O'Hara of Philadelphia recalled being part of "a distinct minority in a town that had more than its share of bigots." In his view: "The wounds received, especially the wounds to our pride, helped to form our character."

When the Irish clergyman M. B. Buckley toured America in 1870–1871, he noted in his diary that "the antipathy to the Catholic religion and the Irish population is very intense" and jotted down an example that symbolized the situation. On a carriage drive through the New England countryside, he was shown an ordinary house near "a very stately mansion." An Irishman had built the house near the mansion, much to the outrage of the Yankee owner who was unable to prevent it. As a last resource, the Yankee "erected a long and wooden wall that would completely shut out from view the domicile of the unoffending Patrick." Rev. Buckley saw "the wall of separation" and "could not help feeling disgusted that any man's hatred for another could carry him to such absurd and ridiculous lengths."

In this anti-Irish and anti-Catholic atmosphere, organized opposition had emerged as early as the 1830's. As noted by de Tocqueville, the celebrated French observer of America at that time: "The greatest part of British America was peopled by men who, having shaken off the authority of the Pope, acknowledged no other religious supremacy" and "the Catholic religion has erroneously been regarded as the natural enemy of democracy." A hostile American publication argued: "Our opinion is that the Roman Catholic Church is the most dangerous enemy that the Republic has to encounter, and that those who are within its pale are the most dangerous enemies of the country."

In New York, the Protestant Association was set up to propagandize against Catholicism, and in Massachusetts the General Association of Congregational Churches called upon pastors to save America "from the degrading influence of popery." The Baptist Home Mission and the Western Baptist Educational Association solicited funds to campaign against Catholicism in the Mississippi Valley and in the West.

In Philadelphia, representatives of twelve Protestant denominations formed the American Protestant Association and, on November 22, 1842, signed a constitution that was typical of the anti-Catholic organizations that were springing up. The preamble stated the belief that Catholicism was "in its principles and tendency, subversive of civil and religious liberty, and destructive to the spiritual welfare of men." The goals of the Association were to encourage Protestant ministers to instruct their congregations "on the differences between Protestantism and Popery," to circulate books and tracts "on the various errors of Popery in their history, tendency, and design" and, finally, "To awaken the attention of the community to the dangers which threaten the liberties, and the public and domestic institutions, of these United States from the assaults of Romanism."

By the 1850's, when the infamous Know-Nothing Party was gaining strength, American tolerance had given way "to a blind, misunderstanding hate," according to a leading historian of nativism, Ray Allen Billington. He notes that "probably one writer only slightly distorted common sentiment" when he described the Pope as an "impostor" and the Mother Church as "the mother of abominations," Catholic priests as men "who profess to 'mortify the flesh' by eschewing matrimony and violating nature," nunneries as places "where beauty that was made to bloom and beam on the world is immured and immolated, not to say prostituted." [8]

The Know-Nothings emerged as a secret party dedicated to the proposition that political power must be kept out of immigrant hands, which meant Catholic hands, which meant the Irish primarily and the Germans secondarily. Organized in 1849 as the Order of the Star Spangled Banner, the party got its name because its members avoided any questions regarding their organization by answering, "I know nothing about it." By 1854, the party had built up considerable strength in Maryland, Delaware, Kentucky, and most of New England and had held a convention with delegations from 13 states.

According to its constitution, a member had to be 21 or over, believe in God, be native-born, a Protestant born of Protestants, "reared under Protestant influence, and not united in marriage with a Roman Catholic." Nor was there any subtlety in the oath taken by Know-Nothings to support and vote only for an American-born citizen who is "in favor of American-born ruling America," and specifically not to vote for Roman Catholics.

Besides tapping the reservoir of anti-Catholic, anti-Irish feelings, the Know-Nothings profited from the political confusion of the period as well as reactions against immigrant competition for unskilled jobs. The growing struggle over slavery, the decline of the Whig Party and the reorganization of the Democratic Party left many voters politically adrift. The Know-Nothings offered an alternative and a simplistic issue—nativism—on which many Americans could agree.

In various state elections during 1854 and 1855, the Know-Nothings won important victories on their own or with allies in Delaware, Kentucky, Maryland, and many New England states, including the governorship, all state offices, and practically the entire legislature of Massachusetts. Other victories were chalked up in Tennessee, New York, California, Georgia, Alabama, Mississippi, Louisiana, and Texas. An estimated 75 to 100 Know-Nothings were elected to Congress and the Know-Nothings hoped to put their man in the White House in 1856.

The Know-Nothing candidate for President, Millard Fillmore, did get one-fourth of the votes in 1856, but thereafter the party declined rapidly. Their officeholders made a poor showing, particularly in Massachusetts where their terms were characterized by blunder and scandal. In the U.S. Congress, none of their bills were passed. By the end of the 1850's, the Know-Nothings were political has-beens, withal a vivid personification of the bigotry that spurred Irish Catholics to greater solidarity.

Later in the nineteenth century, their echo was heard when a new anti-Catholic organization mushroomed—the American Protective Association (A.P.A.). Its members took a secret oath against supporting a Roman Catholic for public office and promised never to employ a Catholic as long as a Protestant was available. Foreign-born members were accepted as long as they were anti-Catholic, which implied anti-Irish as well. Founded in 1887 by a German immigrant's son, Henry F. Bowers, the A.P.A. grew to a million members in the early 1890's, and was particularly strong in the Midwest. However, its leadership could not maintain the momentum, local units split off, and in 1896, when the nation was absorbed in the free silver crusade, the A.P.A. faded out.

In line with the attitudes and rhetoric of nineteenth-century bigotry, convents, churches, and polling places were focal points for rioting. They personified the Irish presence in the United States, which was itself a club-swinging, stone-throwing, head-cracking country. The decades before, during, and after the major influx of the Irish—the 1830's, 1840's, and 1850's—were literally riotous years. Historian Richard Maxwell Brown has described it as "a period of sustained urban rioting, particularly in the great cities of the Northeast" where he counted at least 35 "major riots" in Baltimore, Philadelphia,

New York, and Boston. Other riots occurred in the Midwest and lower Mississippi Valley, particularly in Chicago and Cincinnati.

Brown suggests that the period "may have been the era of the greatest urban violence that America has ever experienced." It was not class warfare as in Europe, but strife caused by the explosive mixing of native Americans and newcomers, namely Irish Catholics and Germans. As the slavery crisis intensified, racial trouble was added to ethnic and religious turmoil. America's "melting pot" was constantly boiling over.

As early as 1831, St. Mary's Church in New York City had been set afire. Other incidents in the pre-Civil War period ranged from church bombings in Dorchester, Massachusetts, and Shelby County, Ohio, to mob action in Bath, Maine, where at the laying of a church cornerstone, a cross was pulled down and an American flag hoisted in its place. Conditions were such in New England that insurance companies refused to cover Catholic churches unless built of nonflammable materials.

For Irish Catholics throughout the country, the burning of a convent near Boston in 1834 symbolized the hostility they faced. Rioters in Charlestown acted out anti-Catholic, anti-Irish emotions against an imposing, brick-red Ursuline convent that stood on Mount Benedict Hill next to historic Bunker Hill and faced Boston across the Charles River. A Catholic historian of the period has called it "the most disgraceful outrage ever perpetrated in New England." For many years thereafter, the burning of the Ursuline convent figured prominently in pro- and anti-Catholic propaganda.

For some time prior to the burning, religious, ethnic, and class tensions had been growing with the steady increase of Irish immigrants. The convent was denounced as "wholly foreign," founded by "foreigners," built with "foreign money," and run "by the spiritual subjects of a foreign potentate, the Pope." The flash point came after one of the nuns, Sister Mary

John, suffered a breakdown, left, and then returned to the convent.

Inflammatory rumors spread throughout the community. Though the nun had returned freely and was remaining voluntarily, reports circulated that she was being held against her will. Eventually, the entire body of Charlestown selectmen visited her to confirm that she wanted to stay in the convent. But by then, feelings had gone beyond a point of recall and so had a plot to burn down the convent. On the day before the burning, a Sunday, a call to arms was sounded in a handbill that appeared in Charlestown: "To Arms!! Ye brave and free. The avenging sword unshield!! Leave not one stone upon another of that curst Nunnery that prostitutes female virtue and liberty under the garb of Holy Religion. When Bonaparte opened the Nunneries in Europe he found cords of infant skulls!!!!!"

The burning and sacking began at midday. As described by a contemporary account:

> Three or four torches, which were or precisely resembled engine torches, were then brought up from the road and immediately upon their arrival, the rioters proceeded into every room in the building, rifling every drawer, desk and trunk which they found, and breaking up and destroying all the furniture, and casting much of it from the windows, sacrificing in their brutal fury, costly piano fortes and harpes, and other valuable instruments. . . . and even the vessels and symbols of christian worship.
>
> After having thus ransacked every room in the building, they proceeded with great deliberation, about one o'clock, to make preparation for setting fire to it. For this purpose, broken furniture, books, curtains and other combustible materials, were placed in the centre of several of the rooms; and, as if in mockery of God as well as of man, the Bible was cast, with shouts of exultation, upon the pile first kindled; and as upon this were subsequently thrown the vestments used in religious

service, and the ornaments of the altar, these shouts and yells were repeated. Nor did they cease until the Cross was wrenched from its place, and cast into the flames, as the final triumph of this fiend-like enterprise.[9]

The bloodiest anti-Catholic anti-Irish rioting erupted in Philadelphia in a characteristic scenario. Immigrant Catholics had moved into the city's industrial perimeter in the 1820's and 1830's and clashed with native American Protestants living in central Philadelphia. There were election riots, fights between volunteer fire companies, and ethnic and religious disputes. The triggering event was a dispute over use of the Protestant Bible in the public schools. Bishop Francis P. Kenrick, a native of Dublin and leader of the city's Catholics since 1830, persuaded the Philadelphia school board in 1842 to permit Catholic children to read the Catholic Douay version of the Bible, thereby setting off Protestant agitation and protests.

The climax came in May, 1844, when Protestants marched into the Irish suburban stronghold of Kensington to hold protest meetings. The Irish dispersed them on May 3 and 6, but in the second confrontation an 18-year-old demonstrator carrying an American flag was mortally wounded. Overnight, a hero and martyr was born. On May 7, a procession of two to three thousand Protestants returned, carrying the victim's flag and a large sign announcing: THIS IS THE FLAG WHICH WAS TRAMPLED UPON BY THE IRISH PAPISTS.

Kensington burned. The protesters hunted armed Irishmen and set houses afire. Non-Catholics saved their homes by putting up signs that read, "No Popery Here" or by displaying a nativist newspaper. Rioting, arson, and violence filled the Philadelphia night: 40 dead, 60 seriously wounded, 81 homes destroyed as well as two Catholic churches, two rectories, two convents, and a Catholic library. The target was Irish Catholicism. No attack was made upon a German Catholic Church.

In early July, more rioting erupted, this time centered

around the Church of St. Philip de Neri where the pastor was storing guns. When word got out of the gun cache, crowds of nativists gathered in front of the church. The state militia held them back temporarily, but then a shooting battle broke out involving the demonstrators, Irish volunteers—the Hibernia Greens—and the militia. Thirteen persons were killed and more than 50 wounded.

Only the intervention of the militia prevented further rioting and attacks on Catholic churches. "For weeks a heavy gloom hung over Philadelphia," remembered a Catholic who witnessed the riots as a boy. "The city was still under martial law and the streets leading to the Catholic churches being guarded by soldiers. . . ." He recalled that "rumor, busy jade, caused many a heart to beat in dread, and many a head to bow in prayer."

Thirty years later, he described a close call he had had while at Sunday Mass with his sisters at a church adjoining embattled St. Philip's. The recollection recaptures the feelings of devotion mixed with the sense of danger that went with being Catholic and Irish during times of rioting. He was engrossed in the Mass when, at the elevation of the Communion host, "the startling clamor of an approaching mob was heard" and "many a rosy countenance assumed the hue of the lily."

He noticed that most of the men in the church rose quietly, without disrupting the celebration of the Mass, and stationed themselves next to the church door. "Nearer and nearer came the cries. . . . Nearer and nearer came the shouts, but the celebrant, if he felt any fear, showed none, as the God of battles lay before him. Nearer and nearer yet came the yells, and as they passed behind the church the solemn *miserere nobis* was over, and the soothing *dona nobis pacem* of Di Monti in D floated melodiously upon our anxious ears. Further and further receded the tumult and when the *Ite missa est* was chanted all was still." [10]

The political counterpart to attacks on churches and convents was violence at polling places, a favorite tactic of the Know-Nothings for frightening off foreign-born voters. Pitched battles were fought by them against the Irish in Philadelphia, Newark, Baltimore, Brooklyn, St. Louis, Chicago, Louisville, and Chelsea and Lawrence, Massachusetts. Baltimore became known as "mob town" for its election-day riots, while in Louisville many Irish and Germans moved out of the city following its "Bloody Monday" riot in 1855. In the latter episode, Know-Nothings captured the polls and, while police and local officials looked the other way, pulled immigrants off voting lines and beat them. As gunfights spread throughout Louisville, 20 persons were killed and a large number injured.

The nativists were not confronting pacifists, however. The Irish had been demonstrating their own penchant for violence, brawling in the cities and protesting management abuses with labor riots in the mines and railroads. The Irish also organized militia companies, a practice common among immigrant groups but pronounced among the Irish. These military units were mainly social and a great excuse for parties, dinners, and rhetoric-drenched speeches. They were also highly visible since the units loved to parade whenever they had a chance. New York had the Emmett Guards, the Irish-American Guard, and the Mitchel Light Guard; Brooklyn boasted the Shields Guard. Compared with German companies which totaled 1,700 in 1853, the Irish had 2,600 militiamen. Philadelphia had the Hibernia Guards which were called out in the 1844 rioting, Boston the Montgomery Guards, the Columbian Artillery, the Bay State Artillery, and the Sarsfield Guards. Other Irish units were the Jasper Greens, Jackson Guards, Irish Rifles, and the Napper Tandy Light Artillery. Such units were formed even in smaller towns, evoking considerable newspaper comment about their penchant for parading.

The greatest demonstration of green power came, appropriately, in New York where Irish Catholics had a fighting prelate to their liking, Bishop John Hughes (later the city's first archbishop). He was militant, domineering, defiant, with a background rooted in his native county of Tyrone and in Pennsylvania where he worked as a day laborer and gardener before entering the seminary. He had built many churches and was determined to protect them in the face of fears that Philadelphia's anti-Catholic riots of 1844 would spread to New York.

Bishop Hughes warned that "if a single Catholic Church were burned in New York, the city would become a second Moscow." As to the Catholics of Philadelphia, "they should have defended their churches since the authorities could not or would not do it for them." When Bishop Hughes met with Mayor Robert H. Morris, he was asked by the mayor if he feared "that some of your churches will be burned." Hughes warned, instead, of what might happen to Protestant churches: "No, sir; but I am afraid that some of *yours* will be burned. We can protect our own. I come to warn you for your own good."

Hughes organized a militant defense system for New York's churches: each was to be occupied by an armed force of one to two thousand men "resolved, after taking as many lives as they could in defence of their property, to give up, if necessary, their own lives for the same cause." When public officials asked Hughes to restrain New York's Irish, he replied: "I have not the power; you must take care that they are not provoked." There were no outbreaks in New York and, as Hughes' admiring biographer John R. G. Hassard recalled in 1866: "The Bishop publicly claimed the merit of having prevented an outbreak." [11]

By mid-century, Bishop Hughes was already demonstrating that the Irish belonged to a church of power as well as piety. In a hostile environment, the Irish had a headquarters that led and protected while also nourishing emotionally. And if the power of their Church could not always protect, the force of their faith offered the solace summarized in 1848 by one

Kathleen Kennedy of Boston: "When we luck at him there, we see our blissed Saviour, stripped a'most naked lake ourselves; whin we luck at the crown i'thorns on the head, we see the Jews mockin' him, jist the same as—some people mock ourselves for our religion; whin we luck at his eyes, we see they wor niver dry, like our own; whin we luck at the wound in his side, why we think less of our own wounds an' bruises, we get 'ithin and 'ithout, every day av our lives." [12]

VI

Catholic Like No One Else

I N A M E R I C A , the Catholic Church flowered in a variety of styles—"the intensely sentimental Catholicism of Spain, the fiercely Puritanical Catholicism of Ireland, the relaxed and affectionate Catholicism of Italy, the reasonable and sophisticated Catholicism of France, the deeply devotional Catholicism of Hungary and Poland." [1]

But no immigrant group took Catholicism more personally than the Irish, was more involved with the Church or more closely tied to the clergy. The Irish not only made Catholicism an integral part of their experience in America, but soon came to dominate the Church organization and its hierarchy. The process was a natural continuation of their religious experience in Ireland, a partnership of poverty and persecution in the old country, a synthesis of traditional piety and new power in America. The Roman Catholic Church was Holy Mother Church for Irish immigrants. They never forgot that, and never let anyone else do so either. [2]

85

As proclaimed by Bishop John Lancaster Spalding, a leading figure in the Catholic hierarchy of the late nineteenth and early twentieth centuries, "No other people could have done for the Catholic faith in the United States what the Irish people have done." In urging the Irish to go West for their own good and for the good of their Church, Spalding (not an Irishman himself) enumerated Irish characteristics important to any religious shepherd tending a flock: "unalterable attachment to their priests, their deep Catholic instincts . . . the unworldly and spiritual temper of the national character; their indifference to ridicule and contempt, and their unfailing generosity." Thus, the Irish accomplished "what would not have been accomplished by Italians, French, or German Catholics." [3]

The Irish had come over with a special bond with their Church. Unlike the Catholic Church in continental Europe, the Irish Church, clergy, and adherents had been outcasts together. Catholicism in Ireland was not part of an oppressive power structure in which princes and priests marched together in religious pomp and political circumstance. Instead, peasant and priest suffered side by side in embattled Ireland, struggling together against all that was English and Protestant. Irish and Catholic were merged into one identity as was the British and Protestant enemy (denoted by the same Irish word for both—*Sassenach*). A leading student of Irish nationalism, Thomas N. Brown, has noted that "perhaps the greatest difficulty which confronts the historian of the Irish is that of differentiating between the specifically Irish and specifically Catholic aspect of their lives." [4]

Coming off the boat, Irish immigrants turned to priests of their own kind and found advice and leadership as well as spiritual nourishment. At birth, marriage, and death, the Irish turned most fervently to their priests and even those who did not attend church regularly made contributions to build churches, schools, hospitals, orphanages, and almshouses.

The triumphal certainty of Irish Catholicism was epitomized in a letter that John Boyle O'Reilly wrote to a friend in the American West. O'Reilly admonished his friend that "a great, loving, generous heart will never find peace and comfort and field of labor except within her unstatistical, sun-like, benevolent motherhood. . . . Man never made anything so like God's work as the magnificent, sacrificial, devotional faith of the hoary but young Catholic Church. There is no other church; they are all just way stations." [5]

The Irish, having no doubts about the importance of their Church in this world and the next, poured energy, money, and fervor into raising it to heights of glory in America. Looking back from the mid-twentieth century at what Irish immigrants had accomplished, social scientists Nathan Glazer and Daniel P. Moynihan cited the transformation of the Catholic Church "from a despised and proscripted sect of the eighteenth century to the largest religious organization of the nation." They called it "incomparably the most important thing they [the Irish] have done in America";[6] historian George Potter has called it their "greatest collective achievement." [7]

In America, the Irish changed what could be described as a cramped chapel for the handful into a splendid cathedral for the immigrant masses. In the original Thirteen Colonies, less than one percent of the three million people were Catholic. Then the increase began: from 35,000 Catholics in 1790 to 90,000 in 1815, to 160,000 in 1830, to more than 300,000 in 1829 when the First Provincial Council of Baltimore was held. On the eve of the Irish transformation of the American Catholic Church, the U.S. bishops at the Council sent a letter, on October 24, 1829, to Pope Pius VIII reflecting the optimism that was so contagious in America: "We see so many blessings bestowed by God on these rising churches, such increase given to this vineyard, that those who planted and those who watered, and those who harvested and tread the over-flowing wine-press, are compelled to confess and wholly admire the finger of God."

The first contribution of the Irish to their Church was numbers. In the 1840's alone, half a million Irish Catholics arrived in America; in the 1860's, 600,000. Overall, between 1840 and 1880, the number of American Catholics increased tenfold—from 600,000 to over six million. The Catholic Church at mid-nineteenth century struggled to keep up: five archbishops, 24 bishops, and only 2,000 priests to serve the flood of newly-arrived Catholics, to satisfy their religious needs, and to put a roof over their religious services.

From a mission station in Saugerties, New York, Father P. J. M. Reilly described the "zeal which I saw the poor creatures manifest in attendance in the services of their religion" and he made a resolution common to thousands of priests in America: "When I saw them enter my temporary little place of worship, from their homes beyond the Catskills, on the morning of Sunday, pale, wayworn, and fasting, having travelled all the night of Saturday, I thought I would build a church which would be to them a bond of union, and a resting place, around whose walls they might deposit in sacred security the mortal remains of their kindred, with the deep, enduring affection of Ireland, which buries its heart in the 'grave with those it loves.'" [8]

Across the country, the Catholic Church was creating a structure to match its expansion. By 1850, 32 dioceses were in operation, doubling the total in ten years. Whereas in 1840 Dubuque had been the frontier diocese, in 1850 the Pacific Coast had three sees. A coast-to-coast foundation was being laid, if a rudimentary one, as in Little Rock where a diocese was established for an estimated 700 Catholics, served by a bishop, one priest, and two churches that were heavily in debt. Meanwhile, between 1840 and 1850, the number of priests quadrupled and the number of churches and mission stations doubled, as did the total number of ecclesiastical institutions (29), colleges (17), and academies for girls (91).

While the Irish were not the only immigrant group providing large numbers of Catholics, as the first major influx they soon dominated the church hierarchy. Between 1789 and 1935, 268 of the 464 U.S. bishops were born in Ireland or were sons of Irish immigrants. (This does not include third-generation Irish bishops.) In 1886, of the 69 bishops in the United States, 35 were Irish; the Germans came second with only 15. "The Germans are a pillar of the Church in America, but the Irish have always held the rooftop," Sir Shane Leslie noted in the *Dublin Review* of August 1918.*

For the Irish, the rise up the hierarchical ladder often progressed from pick and cap to mitre and crosier. Humble origins made for strong ties between the Irish and their bishops and cardinals. So it was that the redoubtable Bishop Hughes, a day laborer before entering the seminary, chose to spend the eve of his episcopal consecration with a laborer he once worked with, declining invitations from well-to-do Catholics. The celebrated Bishop John Ireland had come over with his family after the famine struck and grew up in Minnesota where his father was a carpenter. The successful missionary bishop Matthew Anthony O'Brien, one of a distiller's 13 children, worked his way to America. Boston's Bishop John Williams was the son of an Irish blacksmith—"an industrious and hard-working man, whose physique was of the kind developed at the forge." Rochester's first bishop, Bernard John McQuaid, was still a boy when his father was killed in a fight with a fellow laborer. The first U.S. cardinal, John McCloskey,

* The Irish dominance has persisted into the 1970's, with the Irish comprising 17 percent of the Catholic population, but 35 percent of the priesthood and 50 percent of the hierarchy. By contrast, the Italians, with 19 percent of the Catholic population, are the largest ethnic group in the church, but constitute only 5 percent of the clergy and a mere 3 percent of the hierarchy. (Andrew M. Greeley, *Priests in the United States* [Garden City, N.Y.: Doubleday & Co., 1972], p. 17.)

also lost his father early in life, and went to school on the charity of local priests, as did the second cardinal, James Gibbons. William Cardinal O'Connell of Boston was a canal laborer's son; the sixth U.S. cardinal, Denis Joseph Dougherty, came out of the Pennsylvania coal mines.

Second-generation Irish clergy were continuously reinforced by the direct export of missionary priests from Ireland. They went where their countrymen went, including embryonic dioceses in the Far West. After gold was discovered in California in 1848, Catholics joined the rush and added to the exploding population of San Francisco (which jumped from 800 in 1848 to 25,000 two years later and kept booming). Chapels run by missionaries in the area could in no way deal with their religious needs so the Catholic Church in San Francisco embarked on an impressive building boom of its own. On June 17, 1849, a wooden shanty on a newly-purchased lot was blessed and mass celebrated in it; 30 years later, the Diocese of San Francisco had 133 churches, 16 chapels, five colleges, four asylums, five hospitals, and 128 priests serving 180,000 Catholics.

One of the best-known Irish missionaries in the United States, Father Eugene O'Connell, went to San Francisco to help Bishop Joseph S. Alemany cope with the situation. He described what he found in a letter to Father Moriarity, the head of his seminary, All Hallows College, Dublin, which supplied more missionary priests than any other institution in Ireland. The letter, dated June 15, 1853, cited the bishop's "urgent need" of Irish clergymen and his effort to build a "fire-proof church in the neighborhood, that he himself and his clergymen may be without the daily and nightly apprehension of being *burnt out*." Then he provided a glimpse of the "iniquity" abounding—"the rage for duelling, the passion for gambling and barefaced depravity prevail to a frightful degree. . . . Venus has numerous temples erected to herself in this city, but, thank God, the Catholic church is not deserted all the while. The two Catholic churches are crowded every Sunday. . . ." [9]

Religious orders of women also went West as part of the out-reach of Ireland's convents. Over the decades, they were joined by American-born recruits, thereby increasing the monumental contribution of religious women to education and to every kind of social welfare. Histories of the Catholic Church tend to pay limited attention to them, and, as church historian John Tracy Ellis notes, "for the most part their striking contributions have gone unrecorded." [10]

Among the Irish orders, the Sisters of Mercy came to Pittsburgh in the 1840's, spread eastward to New York and New England, then went to Omaha, Nebraska, in 1846. The state was still Indian country, the town no more than an outpost when, at the invitation of Bishop James Myles O'Gorman of Omaha, seven Sisters of Mercy arrived via steamboat at the "strange, wild-looking place." The flavor of the nineteenth-century missionary experience emerges from a contemporary account, a mixture of good humor, hardship, and indefatigable faith. The band of nuns spent their first night in a three-story brick house that had schoolrooms on the second floor and a dormitory on the third, which looked like "a huge stable" with its partitioned sleeping quarters. The entire house had "absolutely nothing but a stove and a piano," which meant the nuns had to sleep on the floor. Faced with such stark surroundings, the younger nuns "amused" themselves by facetiously asking for all sorts of luxuries in a "situation so ridiculous that they laughed themselves to sleep."

Breakfast on the first morning involved bribing a young boy to bring them some wood in exchange for the chance to see a piano. "Two Sisters had to trudge across the prairie to a sort of a farm house to buy milk. A boy kindly went for bread. Tin cups were borrowed. The Sisters sat on the floor about the stove and stirred their coffee Japanese fashion, with chop sticks, picked up under the carpenter's shed. Later in the day, a wealthy lady supplied some of their more pressing wants. The best room was cleaned out for a chapel. A box lined with linen and gold paper became the tabernacle. The Bishop said Mass the first Sunday, the piano doing duty for an altar." [11]

The abiding contribution of Irish women to Catholicism was the steadfast piety that was popularly celebrated—a singular model and a strong influence in the family. In Maguire's nineteenth-century description, the Irish woman was "naturally religious," her fervor turned to "devotional enthusiasm," and she filled her leisure with religious practices and activities. It is a convincing portrayal that undoubtedly affected upcoming generations, particularly the Irish sons and daughters who fulfilled their mothers' dreams by becoming priests and nuns. As Maguire continued his description of the Irish-Catholic woman:

> If she happens to be in a new mission, where everything— church, school, asylum, hospital—is to be erected, she enters into the holy task with congenial ardour. To build up, finish, or decorate a church—to her, the House of God and Temple of her Ancient Faith—she contributes with generous hand. It is the same in a long-established parish, whose spiritual necessities keep pace with its growing population; there, also, the Irish girl is unfailing in her liberality. To her there is no idea of making a sacrifice of her means; she gives as well as a pleasure as from a feeling of duty. . . . Thus is maintained over her that religious control which is her own best preservative against danger, and which, while forming and strengthening her character, enables her to bring a salutary influence to bear upon her male relatives, and in case of her marriage—a contingency most probable— upon her husband and children.[12]

In Cardinal O'Connell's recollections of his boyhood, his mother emerged as one such Irish woman who "lived and thought and worked and walked perpetually in the light of God's holy presence." The day began "with prayer at her knee," continued "with constant reminders of God's care and love and providence" and ended in the evening with recitation of the Rosary, "which all the children, no matter what their age, were bound to attend." The future Cardinal, born December 8, 1859, felt that as the youngest among several children he was under his mother's influence more than his brothers and sisters, and he saw his mother as retaining "to the end in my eyes wonderful beauty of character and expression." [13]

Rose Fitzgerald Kennedy, herself a model of religious devotion, recalled in her autobiography where she had received her own "precious gift of faith." As she grew up in the 1890's and early 1900's, "the Church was a pervading and abiding presence" in her mother's life and "she instilled these feelings in us." Her mother drilled the children in their cathechism and other religious tenets and talked of religious feasts and the various holy seasons. "May was the month of the Blessed Virgin," Rose Kennedy wrote in *Times to Remember*. "There was a little shrine to her in our house, with her statue, and all month we kept it decorated with fresh flowers and offered a prayer there each night. Every night during Lent my mother would gather us in one of the rooms of the house, turn out the lights—the better to concentrate—and lead us in reciting the Rosary." [14]

While Irish men were hardly as pious and devoted as their women, they dramatized their commitment to their faith during the U.S. Civil War, when large numbers of Irish soldiers went into battle. Bravery and benedictions went hand in hand. One moment Irish soldiers "knelt down to receive, bareheaded, the benediction of their priest, next moment rushed into the fray with a wilder cheer and a more impetuous dash." [15]

An Irish chaplain named Father Sheeran recalled the Christmas morning when the snow was so heavy that he lost his way to the place where he was to celebrate mass. When he finally arrived, he saw a crowd of whitened figures crowded around a little tent in which an altar had been set up. It was the only clear spot as icy winds swirled heavy snows all about, and the Irish regiment stood as solemnly as any congregation, though they were on the edge of battle.

In his further accounts celebrating the Irish in America, Maguire reported a conversation with "a distinguished colonel, of genuine American race" who said that at first he had laughed in his sleeve at the religious piety of Irish soldiers. "The fact is—you will pardon me—I thought it all so much damned tomfoolery and humbug. That was at first, sir. But I found the most pious of them the very bravest—and that astonished me more than anything. Sir, I saw these men tried in every way that men could be tried, and I never saw anything superior to them. Why, sir, if I wanted to storm the gates of hell, I didn't want any finer or braver fellows than those Irishmen. . . . I saw them in battle, sir; but I also saw them sick and dying in the hospital, and how their religion gave them courage to meet death with cheerful resignation." On the victorious note with which Irish Catholics liked to round out such stories, the colonel converted to Catholicism.[16]

At Gettysburg, on the second day of that devastating battle of 1863, Union general St. Clair Mulholland watched "one of the most impressive religious ceremonies" he had ever seen. Just before the Irish Brigade went into action, they massed in columns to receive a general absolution from their chaplain, Father William Corby.

> Father Corby stood upon a large rock in front of the brigade, addressing the men. . . . The brigade was standing at "order arms," and as he closed his address, every man fell on his knees, with head bowed down. Then, stretching his right hand towards the brigade, Father Corby pronounced the words of absolution. The scene was more than impressive, it was awe-inspiring. Near by stood Gen. Hancock, surrounded by a brilliant throng of officers, who had gathered by to witness this very unusual occurrence, and while there was profound silence in the ranks

of the second corps, yet over to the left, out by the Peach Orchard and Little Round Top . . . the roar of the battle rose and swelled and re-echoed through the woods. The act seemed in harmony with all the surroundings. I do not think there was a man in the brigade who did not offer up a heart-felt prayer. For some it was their last; they knelt there in their grave-clothes—in less than half an hour many of them were numbered with the dead of July 2d.[17]

The civilian counterpart of this piety could be seen any Sunday morning in the cities where Irish Catholics clustered. As journalist James D. McCabe reported in his 1872 account of New York City life, Catholics were "one of the strongest, if not the strongest denomination in the city," their membership consisted "principally of the poorer classes," and the attendance at their churches was "immense." He cited St. Stephen's, on Twenty-eighth Street, between Third and Lexington Avenues, as having a "very large and very beautiful" interior that seated nearly 4,000 and was "usually crowded." [18]

It was St. Stephen's that Protestant observer James Parton selected for a detailed description of "Our Roman Catholic Brethren." He was there for 6 A.M. mass on the cold Sunday morning of December 8, 1867, as the worshippers silently filled the church, waiting for the priest who was late on that particular day. Not a sound was heard, except for the coughing of the chilled congregation. Then the priest entered, accompanied by two altar boys in long red robes, and knelt before the altar. "All present, except one poor heathen in the middle aisle, shuffled to their knees with a pleasant noise, and remained kneeling for some time. The silence was complete. . . . He rose, he knelt, he ascended the steps of the altar, he came down again, he turned his back to the people, he turned his face to them, he changed from one side of the altar to the other, he made various gestures with his hands—but he uttered not an audible word. . . . the people sat, stood, knelt, bowed, and crossed themselves in accordance with the ritual.

But still not a word was spoken. At the usual time the collection was taken, to which few gave more than a cent, but to which *every one* gave a cent."

Later in the mass, after prayers were requested for three deceased parishioners, the service was continued in silence, except for "the gong-like bell, which announced by a single stroke the most solemn acts of the mass." During the "intense stillness" which followed the sound of the bell, "a low, eager whisper of prayer could occasionally be heard, and the whole assembly was lost in devotion." At communion time, about 20 women and five men came forward and soon afterward "some of the women began to hurry away, as if fearing the family at home might be ready for breakfast before breakfast would be ready for them."

As Parton noted, this was but the beginning of that Sunday's worship and a succession of impressive turnouts:

> At ten minutes to seven the priest put on his black cap, and withdrew; and soon the congregation was in full retreat. But by this time another congregation was assembling for the seven o'clock mass; the people were pouring in at every door, and hurrying along all the adjacent streets towards the church. Seven o'clock being a much more convenient time than six, the church is usually filled at that hour; as it is, also, at the nine-o'clock mass. At half past ten the grand mass of the day occurs, and no one who is in the habit of passing a Catholic church on Sunday mornings at that hour needs to be informed that the kneeling suppliants who cannot get in would make a tolerable congregation of themselves.[19]

In regard to life hereafter, the Catholic Irish felt that though the Protestants may have had a better time of it on earth, the Catholics had a postponed, but eternal reward awaiting them. This attitude was epitomized in a story written by Archbishop Hughes as a young man: *The Conversion and Edifying Death of Andrew Dunn.* The hero turns for enlightenment on

Catholicism to "John Smith, a neighbor of his, and a very good liver, but a Roman Catholic." Smith tells him that "the Catholic religion is the safest to die in" and goes on to explain it thus:

> Now it is a certain fact that thousands upon thousands of Protestants, on their deathbeds, call for the assistance of Catholic Priests, and embrace the Catholic Faith; whilst it is equally certain that *no* Catholic, that is no person who had lived all his life-time a Catholic, was ever known to wish to die a Protestant; therefore, Andrew, I think this conclusion clear: the Catholic religion is the *safest and best.*
>
> Again, whilst we see thousands of Protestants daily becoming Catholics, though, by doing so, they are exposed to the ridicule and persecutions of the ungodly; yet we seldom see or hear of any Catholic becoming Protestant unless with a view to live a more unrestrained and licentious life.[20]

On the parish level, many a young Irishman grew up in America under the hard-and-fast attitudes of an Irish country priest. These priests were taken out of Ireland, but Erin's attitudes were by no means taken out of them, particularly the horror of Protestantism. A Catholic doctor looking back on his boyhood in the 1890's recalled the time Father Dan spotted him playing with Protestant friends: "Remember, Owen, that you'll never see any of those lads in another world unless you should offend God and be sent to hell." At another time, he turned on him and said: "And here's Owen that never plays with any good Catholic boys!" This was the youthful Owen's recollected reaction:

"This was not just a big man in a black vest speaking, but the Church. There is no good in trying to explain how this one sentence, just a slap at my mother underhand, drove me into Irish patriotism. I turned my twelve-year-old back on all my Protestant friends and associated exclusively with the Irish."

How did young Owen feel about the priest? "I dreaded him,

and his sermons in Lent scared me into a nervous misery although I was not in the least a sensitive child. You can find how he talked about hell and purgatory in Joyce's first novel." [21]

The Irish were as loyal in religion as in politics. If they heeded their clergy, they revered their hierarchy. The chain of command held firm, stretching from Rome to America, as Bishop Spalding proudly remarked in 1880: "Pius IX, it is reported, was accustomed to say that only in America was he truly Pope." Bishop Spalding noted that the Pope "meets with no hindrance whatever in this country" and it was the same with American bishops "who have the fullest freedom in the exercise of their high office." Spalding added that the "Catholic bishops are the only class of men in the republic who exercise real power and at the same time hold office for life." [22]

Fortunately for the Americanization of the Irish and their religion, a consummate diplomat, James Gibbons, emerged to lead the Catholic Church in America. Tolerant, flexible, and statesmanlike, he became in 1867 at the age of 34 the "boy bishop" of North Carolina. Appropriately, when he was three years old, his mother Bridget from County Mayo had held him high to see Andrew Jackson, the son of poor Irish immigrants, march by as president of the United States. In his career—bishop for 53 years, Archbishop of Baltimore for 44 years, and Cardinal for 35 years—Gibbons became the voice of reason and harmony within the Catholic Church, and outside it as well. In addition, he wrote what Catholic historian Theodore Maynard called "the most stupendous Catholic 'best-seller' ever to be written in English." [23] Cardinal Gibbons would later, with characteristic benevolence, note: "Of all things about the book (*Faith of Our Fathers*), the point that gratifies me most is that, although it is an explanation of the Catholic religion, there is not one word in it that can give offence to our Protestant brethren." It was a long way, psychologically and historically, from Archbishop Hughes' *The Conversion and*

Edifying Death of Andrew Dunn to Cardinal Gibbons' *Faith of Our Fathers.*

In 1887, when Gibbons went to Oregon to install a new archbishop soon after he himself had become the second U.S. Cardinal, the trip turned into a triumphant tour. It symbolized his success as the acknowledged leader of the American Catholic Church and the strides made by immigrant Catholics. "Reports from points en route," the editor of the Baltimore *Catholic Mirror* told his readers, "indicate that the beloved head of the Church in America has been everywhere received with the strongest tokens of affectionate respect and esteem by all classes of citizens without regard to creed."

By that time, the U.S. Catholic population was approaching nine million. Decade by decade, the growth remained impressive: over 3 million in 1860, 4.5 million in 1870, six and a quarter million in 1880, 8.9 million in 1890. (By the close of the century, almost one in six Americans was Catholic.) The Church tried to keep pace, but the clergy remained a Gideon's army numbering in the mere thousands for a Catholic population in the millions. In 1870, there were 3,780 priests; in 1880, 6,000; in 1890, 9,000.

Gibbons did not hesitate to credit the Irish immigrants, for instance, in an 1870 St. Patrick's Day sermon: "Is not this country chiefly indebted to her [Ireland] for its faith? There are few churches erected from Maine to California, from Canada to Mexico which Irish hands have not helped to build, which Irish purses have not supported, and in which Irish hearts are not found worshipping. She contributes not only to the *materiel* but also to the *personnel* of the Church in this country. A large proportion of our Bishops and clergy are of Irish origin or descent."

The truth of this last statement caused much friction among the growing numbers of German-Americans who comprised the largest single immigrant group in the second half of the century. Just as the Irish had earlier resented the French-dominated hierarchy, so now the German immigrants—half of them Catholics—resented Irish domination. Their resentment culminated in a controversial demand that the American Church be reorganized according to nationality. Instead of dioceses with geographical boundaries, aroused German-Catholics wanted divisions along ethnic lines and the appointment of bishops to match the proportion of Catholics from each nationality. This would have effectively divided power in the American Catholic Church of the 1880's between the Germans and the Irish, and certified the ethnic hyphenation of Catholics.

The effort failed. It was at odds with the movement toward Americanizing Catholicism and with the Irish directorate of the Catholic Church. The proposal for an ethnic reorganization of the American church was embodied in a document called the Lucerne Memorial, prepared by European representatives of the St. Raphael Societies of Europe, which were concerned with German migration to the United States. It was delivered to the Pope by the leading figure behind the proposal, Peter Paul Cahensly.

One Irish bishop wrote to Cardinal Gibbons that "to your Eminence we must look for salvation from the wicked wretch, Cahensly, who is striving to undo the work of the Church in our country." The fiery Archbishop of St. Paul, John Ireland (born in Kilenny, Ireland), described the proposal as the "Lucerne conspiracy" and added that "we are American bishops . . . and effort is made to dethrone us and to foreignize our country in the name of religion." Cardinal Gibbons, with characteristic diplomacy and tact, criticized the Lucerne Memorial without causing a rupture with German Catholics, who meanwhile were able to establish local parishes along ethnic lines. The Pope rejected the Lucerne proposals and the Irish remained on the rooftops of the American church.

Gibbons' stress on the American identity of Catholicism was

in tune with the broader emphasis on Americanizing every aspect of immigrant life. At the time of the controversy, Gibbons had a meeting with President Benjamin Harrison and then made known the President's support for Gibbons' opposition to the Lucerne proposal. The meeting and its outcome demonstrated the power and position of the Catholic Church in the United States. Said Gibbons at the time: "Let us glory in the title of American citizen. We owe our allegiance to one country, and that country is America."

Cardinal Gibbons continued to oversee a growing body of Catholics who reached 17 million in 1917, still one out of six Americans. There were 20,000 priests in 10,190 parishes with 5,687 schools serving 1.5 million children. Upon his death in 1921, Cardinal Gibbons evoked tributes honoring the Americanizing role he had personified. Former President Taft said: "He did not belong to the Catholic Church alone, but he belonged to the country at large. He was Catholic not only in the religious sense, but in the secular sense." Said President Harding: "It was my good fortune to know him personally and I held him in the highest esteem and veneration. His death is a distinct loss to the country."

The final testimonials to Cardinal Gibbons echoed the call of Bishop John England almost 100 years before. Bishop England had advised the Catholics of Charleston, South Carolina: "When upon your approach to the polls, any person addresses you as an Irishman, or a Frenchman, or an Italian, or by any appellation but Carolinian or American, his language is distraint and offensive. He is either ignorant or supposes you to be so, or has some sinister view. There is a BRIBERY OF THE AFFECTIONS."

But in point of fact, bribery was openly offered and affection readily returned as the Irish experience evolved. In no area was this more apparent than in the sphere of American politics where a third label, Democrat, was added to Irish and Catholic.

VII

"Hurrah for Gineral Jackson"

THE IRISH VIRTUALLY ARRIVED in America as Democrats. "Here comes a shipload of Irish," English poet Charles Latrobe wrote as early as the 1830's. "They land upon the wharfs of New York in rags and one-knee'd breeches, with raw looks and bare necks. They flourish their cudgels, throw up their torn hats, and cry, 'Hurrah for Gineral Jackson.' "

The *hurrah* was reflex enthusiasm for "Old Hickory," the son of poor Irish emigrants, the general who had defeated the hated British at New Orleans in the War of 1812, the common man's President elected by the Democratic Party. In Jackson, the Irish had a hero; in his party, they had a style, a point of view, and a political approach to which they responded out of instinct and self-interest. Jacksonian democracy suited the Irish: grass-roots, personalized politics that rewarded the faithful, the loyal, and the regular. Its approach was populist and its policies favored the immigrants.

For the Irish, there was really no contest between the established Whig Party and the haven of the newcomers, the Democratic Party. When Thomas L. Nichols, an American doctor who eventually settled in London, described in 1864 his *Forty Years of American Life*, he noted: "By a kind of instinct the Irish have attached themselves almost universally to the democratic party. They got the idea that it was the party of popular rights, the anti-aristocratic party, the liberal party. They at least knew their friends. The democrats always welcomed and guarded the rights of the foreigner. The Federal-Whig-Republican party always hated foreigners, and wished to restrict their rights of citizenship." [1] In an 1836 commentary, the *Boston Pilot* claimed that the Irish "discriminate with a knowledge almost intuitive" between the two parties.[2]

As the British observer Philip Bagenal noted in 1882, nativism and Know-Nothingism "might almost be described as the vestibule of the present Republican party." [3] The Irish accepted that image of the Republicans and, as a result, their recurring fear of Know-Nothingism helped to maintain their staunch loyalty to the Democrats.

Such was the commitment to the Democrats that an Irish voter who deserted the party was regarded as a traitor to Ireland and an apostate from the Catholic Church. Turning against the political faith of Irish-Americans to vote for a Whig candidate was viewed as heretical. Warned an Irish paper in 1838: Such a wayward voter is "a traitor to his country—an apostate to his faith—and a grovelling slave amidst freemen." [4]

Or as Finley Peter Dunne, the Chicago laureate of Irish-American wit, wrote in his 1901 collection of *Mr. Dooley's Opinions*: "Out here [Chicago] a man that often changes his shirt don't often change his pollytics. A man's in th' same party till he take th' broad jump—an' sometimes aftherward, f'r most iv th' people in this ward wud die befure they'd be burrid by a raypublican undertaker." [5]

In 1865, when the Irish-American newspaper *The Leader* wanted to warn its New York City readers about Republican mayoralty candidate Marshall Roberts, it concluded a political limerick, "The Wearin' of the Green," thus:

> If Roberts should be mayor, sure, our liberties
> would cease;
> The foreign-born would never vote—we'd have a
> black police;
> A more distressful country there never would
> be seen;
> They'd be hanging us for taxes and the Wearin'
> of the Green! [6]

For politicians, whose kingdom rested on the ballot box, the Irish vote was to be courted, pursued, and even propositioned. The Irish set the pattern of ethnic voting that has flourished among all immigrant groups. They were the first to be wooed by statements of friendliness toward American minorities: as the Whig Party nominee for President, Henry Clay, told a St. Patrick's Day dinner gathering in 1832: "Some of my nearest and dearest friends [are] Irishmen."

As the large number of potential Irish votes was recognized, so was enthusiasm for Irish candidates. With obvious distaste, a prominent German immigrant, Francis Lieber, noted in 1835 that the Irish "clan more together than the emigrants of any other nation" and vote "under the banner of Irishmen." It was already clear in the 1830's that "there is no election in any of the large cities without some previous calls upon the 'true born sons of Ireland' to vote so or so." Lieber described election-day banners "floating from the windows of taverns, some of which, you may be certain are ornamented with mottos having reference to the Irish alone." [7]

In New York's mayoralty election of 1867, Horace Greeley's *New York Tribune* epitomized the attempts at "bribery of affections" that were directed toward the Irish-American voter throughout the nineteenth and early twentieth centuries. One particular *Tribune* appeal came unblushing from that Republican source with a maximum amount of Irish-oriented rhetoric:

> The nomination of Fernando Wood and Mr. Hoffman, neither of whom has a drop of Irish blood in his veins, for Mayor of a city, three-fourths of whose Democratic voters are Irish, is an insult to the honor of the Old Sod, which every true Irish Democrat will avenge, if he is not lost to all sense of the glory of the land that bore him. . . . Awake, slumbering sons of old Ireland, and give such a demonstration of your affection for the Irish name and blood as will command the reverence of those miscreants. . . . Why not elect an Irish Mayor, on an exclusively Irish ticket, with a shillilah and a short rope, without benefit of clergy, for the American that ventures to offer to vote for it? Irishmen stand up for your rights and the Mayoralty is yours. . . . Nominate an Irishman, elect an Irishman, and then, when you call upon him in the City Hall, you've got an Irish Mayor as sure as there's never a snake nor a toad in Ireland.[8]

Where the affections of the Irish could not be bribed, their hostility could be aroused as in the celebrated RUM, ROMANISM, AND REBELLION incident. On October 29, 1884, a Protestant clergyman named Samuel D. Burchard established a landmark in the history of ethnic voting in America. He was greeting Republican Presidential candidate James G. Blaine, on the steps of New York's Fifth Avenue Hotel, on behalf of a delegation of Protestant clergymen:

> We are your friends, Mr. Blaine, and notwithstanding the calumnies that have been urged in the papers against you, we stand by your side. We expect to vote for you next Tuesday. . . . We are Republicans, and don't propose to leave our party, and identify ourselves with the party whose antecedents have been RUM, ROMANISM, AND REBELLION. We are loyal to our flag; we are loyal to you.[9]

Blaine could have done without such friends, for the RUM,

ROMANISM, AND REBELLION alliteration cost him the
Presidency. At that point, the Democratic Party was seriously
concerned about losing the accustomed faithfulness of a
half-million Irish voters. In Blaine, the Republicans had a
candidate whose mother was Irish Catholic and whose cousin,
Sister Angela, was described as the mother superior of a
convent (during the campaign, the cousin developed a closer
blood relationship, becoming Blaine's sister). Blaine himself
referred to "the ancient faith in which my mother lived and
died."

Blaine also had an anti-British image derived from his
aggressiveness toward Great Britain while Secretary of State.
In Boston, the Irish Land League claimed that "Ireland would
be free in thirty days" if Blaine were elected, and in New York
leading Irish-Americans led a giant Blaine rally that opened
with these heretical words: "This is one of the most significant
meetings ever held in the city of New York. To think of
thousands of Irish Democrats assembled together to indorse
the nomination of the Republican Party. . . ." [10]

The Democrats had nominated New York's Governor
Grover Cleveland, who was denounced as pro-British because
of his free-trade policy and as a bigoted, anti-Irish, anti-Catholic Presbyterian. The Republicans sent a campaign document
to priests throughout the country, trying to convince them of
the latter, while the Democrats drew on the bishops of Albany
and Buffalo to rebut the document. New York's *Irish American*, a newspaper both militant and loyal to the Democrats,
averred that Cleveland had as good a strain of Irish blood as
Blaine, since the Democrat's mother had been Miss O'Neill
before her marriage. Patrick A. Collins, a leading Boston
Irishman, was invited to the governor's mansion in Albany and,
soon after, delivered a speech in favor of Cleveland. The
Democrats quickly sent around a million copies of the speech
and, for good measure, accused Blaine of past involvement
with Know-Nothings and prohibitionists.

The *Irish American,* working hard to keep its readers regular, attacked Blaine on both religious and political grounds. Blaine was called "the tattooed candidate, who is charged with being a renegade to the faith of his mother, and whose whole political record is a foul blot on the reputation of the Irish race for honor and probity." The paper added that if this is not sufficient to turn the Irish voter against Blaine, "he can rely on the history of the origin of the Republican Party, its unvarying anti-Irish proclivities. . . ." [11]

With the Irish vote—and its effect on this very close race—hanging in the balance, Blaine wound up his campaign in New York. He had every reason to be hopeful, since Irish voters were swinging his way and even Tammany Democrats were lukewarm to Cleveland. (A Tammany leader had told the Democratic nomination convention that "Cleveland cannot carry the State of New York.")

Then Burchard alliterated, and on the following Sunday handbills containing his words were distributed at Catholic churches throughout the country. It worked particularly well in New York where Blaine further hurt his cause among Irish laborers by basking in the honors bestowed upon him by wealthy Republican supporters at a fancy banquet in Delmonico's. On election night, Cleveland carried New York state by a mere 1,149 votes out of 1.67 million cast, with everyone agreeing that Burchard had cost Blaine much more than that in Irish votes. As it turned out, the loss of New York cost Blaine the election and made Cleveland, in 1885, the first Democrat to become President after the Civil War.

On the local level, in particular, the Irish had none of the characteristically Protestant inclination toward moralizing and crusading in politics. The Irish flavor was pragmatic rather than idealistic. The Irish responded in terms of personal interest, of opportunities to be gained, of politicians who would deliver bread-and-butter benefits. Let the well-established Protestants mount moral crusades; the outsider Irish

Catholics concentrated on winning elections. This separated them from the Protestants psychologically as well as politically. The Protestants deigned to dabble in politics with a *noblesse oblige,* holding political office at arm's length. The Irish jumped into the political arena, asking not what they could do for government, but what government, i.e., elected officials, could do for them. (President Kennedy's celebrated statement in the opposite direction was a reflection of how Americanized he could sound under the influence of the Ivy League tradition of Protestant idealism.)

In political competition, the Irish, unlike other immigrant groups, had a command of English (though many Famine immigrants had come from Gaelic-speaking areas) and a ready familiarity with the electoral style of politicking. What was more, America offered them the opportunity to obtain a commodity they had so self-consciously lacked in the old country—power.

So the Irish took to politics in America personally and pragmatically. They were not out to save the world, just themselves. Irish politics was hard-headed and down-to-earth. It was the politics of self-interest, earth-bound rather than Utopian. Anything else, given the realities of Irish urban life, would have been perverse as well as ridiculous. The Church took care of the next world; this one was giving the Irish so much trouble that they were forced to turn to their politicians for help.

So an election was not a moral crusade, but a battle for supremacy. As Edward Ross pointed out in 1914, in Irish eyes, "an election is not the decision of a great impartial jury, but a struggle between the 'ins' and 'outs.' Those who vote the same way are 'friends.' To scratch or to bolt is to 'go back on your friends.' Places and contracts are 'spoils.' The official's first duty is to find berths for his supporters." [12] The consistency of this political ethos has been summarized by the contemporary political commentator, William Shannon, in characterizing John F. Kennedy as the personification of Irish and Catholic political traditions: Irish political machines operated on the "theory that most men act in politics on the basis of immediate interests of which food, clothing, shelter, a job and elementary self-respect are primary. . . . The whole idea that one would lose an election for the sake of an abstract principle is alien to this Irish tradition." [13]

The Irish shaped and directed the big-city political machines in post-Civil War America. In politics, as in religion, their numbers, their strong loyalties, their combativeness, and their energies carried them to domination of the organization. Thus Irish-Americans brought forth bishops and politicians, not by accident, but by the same devotion to power.

As a group, the Irish could be counted upon to be "regulars." Catholic Church on Sunday, Democratic ballots on Election Day. They believed in the organization and they endorsed the hierarchy in rendering both to God and to Caesar. In a scholarly study of the Irish and Irish politicians, Edward M. Levine has underlined the "common attributes" of the Catholic Church and the political party organization. "Each confronted the Irish with sharply defined power structures and authority relationships, and provided them with services they could obtain nowhere else. . . . Since these were the only organizations with which the Irish had contact and to which they had access, each reinforced the character and correctness of the other." [14]

The pyramid of organization ran along parallel lines for church and party. At the top was the bishop of the diocese and the party leader of the county (The Boss), followed by church pastors and Assembly District leaders (ward bosses). The pastor worked with his assistant curates, the ward boss with precinct captains. And in the organizational world beyond, the bishop's line of command went up to the Roman Curia, the

College of Cardinals and the Pope himself; the county leader's to the state and national conventions and to the state and national party.

The epitome of the political machine was Tammany Hall, which ran the Democratic Party in New York City. When "Honest John" Kelly took over from the infamously dishonest Boss Tweed in 1873, he symbolized Irish domination of big-city political machines. Kelly demonstrated the "same genius for organization which made the Irish so successful as leaders in the Church and in the field of labor," as historian Carl Wittke has noted.[15] An admirer said of Kelly that he found Tammany "a horde" and left it "an army."

Like their countrymen in the Church hierarchy, Irish bosses came from the world of pick and cap. "Honest John" Kelly was the son of poor Irish immigrants who settled on New York's Hester Street. The "one and only Mike Walsh," who was defeated by Kelly in 1854 when he sought re-election to Congress, had been brought over as a child from County Cork, and had worked as a printer's apprentice, and as deckhand and fireman on a riverboat before becoming a political boss. Richard Croker, Kelly's successor, had been a machinist, a fireman, and a prize fighter. After Croker came Charles Francis Murphy, up from jobs in factories, saloons and shipyards to rule Tammany from 1902 to 1922. Counterparts of what Wittke called "these amazing New York characters" [16] emerged in big cities from coast to coast: Boston's John F. Fitzgerald, Cleveland's John Farley, Philadelphia's John Campbell, Buffalo's William F. Sheehan, Milwaukee's Timothy ("Father Tim") O'Brien, San Francisco's Christopher A. Buckley, California's David Broderick, New Jersey's James Smith, Chicago's Michael ("Hinky Dink") Kenna.

These sons of poverty created a rough-hewn, self-made aristocracy of power. They won rather than inherited what they had, and the sense of importance they projected was distinctively Irish-American. It was not European pomp and circumstance, nor the general's or admiral's braided trappings, but a subtle panoply of power in the person, in the manner and bearing. It was a *gestalt* of *The Boss*, as detailed in one reporter's 1875 description of Brooklyn's Hugh McLaughlin, the first city politician to be called *Boss:*

> He is six feet and over, his corpulent body representing good living. His shoulders are thrown back as his stomach is thrown forward. His hat is always last year's, with the silk brushed the wrong way. His suit, which is all from the same piece of cloth, is always dingy and unbrushed. . . . His boots are sometimes blacked, but the polish is that of some time before. As seen a block away there is nothing attractive in Mr. McLaughlin's appearance more than in that of any portly six footer. But as he steps among the politicians and finds a pathway ready for him in their midst there is that about the bearing of his round head, and the quiet keen look of his small blue eyes that betrays the leader. As soon as he is within the rotunda he is encompassed by politicians. He stands above them all, erect, uncompromising in his bearing and with a mild yet powerful dignity. His face is good natured, and bears the imprint of his Irish birth: his cheeks are full, fat, and smooth, but not puffy; his forehead slopes back gradually until it goes beyond a peninsula of hair which in boyhood was twisted into curly forelocks. His chin is doubled and clean shaven, but there are little tufts of gray sprinkled whiskers in front of each ear. The upper lip is covered by a short stiff mustache which is growing gray, and which would be long but for the frequent singes that it gets from the cigars that burn to stubs beneath it.
>
> Perhaps, the eye alone, of all the man, by whom so many are controlled, is the only feature that indicates his possession of a leader's power. It is of true Irish blue, but gives forth a clearer, more definite and positive expression than is usual in a genial Irish look. It never betrays itself. The expressions that pass over it are worth observing, for they reflect apparently not what the man thinks, but what he wishes his companions to believe he thinks. The prevailing look is that of a mild, well-poised man. As

the politicians buzz about him the eyes look far, very far away, but the ears drink in everything. If in the flow of talk there is any humor, the Boss gives a low, Jay Gouldish, simpering chuckle, the only unmanly characteristic he has.[17]

Bosses like Hugh McLaughlin instinctively grasped and took advantage of the vacuum in American cities where immigrants poured into a cold, inhospitable environment and had only their own kind to turn to for help. The political machine, along with the Church, provided an organization that delivered desperately-needed assistance: jobs, money, and food in times of crisis, help with the courts in times of trouble, mediation for quarrels and disputes. The immigrant Irish did not want more of the cold comfort meted out in the old country by the established Protestants—what John Boyle O'Reilly called:

> Organized charity, scrimped and iced
> In the name of a cautious, statistical Christ.

With its self-interest politics, born of necessity, the political machine flourished as a service agency which did not have to buy votes. It earned them.

Martin Lomasney, who, beginning in the 1880's, ruled Boston politically for over 30 years, pointed out to muckraker Lincoln Steffens the "rock" on which the political machine stood: "I think there's got to be in every ward somebody that any bloke can come to—no matter what he's done—and get help. Help, you understand; none of your law and your justice, but help." Then Steffens added: "I saw that churches had been built upon that need and that sanctuary service, that it was fundamental, that the political boss and his so-called machine stood upon that rock." [18]

Lomasney, the son of an immigrant Irish tailor, eventually was linked to the greatest Irish political success in America. President Kennedy's maternal grandfather was the Boston politician, John F. Fitzgerald, the "Honey Fitz" after whom the Presidential yacht was named. It was Lomasney whom

"Honey Fitz" called "my political grandfather." From Lomasney, he learned these maxims of city politics: the "great mass of people are interested in only three things: food, clothing, and shelter. . . . the politician who thinks he can get away from the people who made him, usually gets what is coming to him—a swift kick in his political pants." [19]

The temple of this down-to-earth brand of politics was the saloon, the social and political rallying point for Irish-Americans. The neighborhood saloon was to Irish politics what the parish church was to Irish religion. The faithful drank, socialized, and talked politics, and from the ranks of saloon owners came Irish political leaders ranging from precinct leader to The Boss. It was said in New York that the only way to break up a meeting of the Tammany Executive Committee was to open the door and shout, "Your saloon's on fire!"

President Kennedy's paternal grandfather got his start in politics as bartender, host, and proprietor of an East Boston saloon, Rose Kennedy recalls in her autobiography. P. J. Kennedy "found himself in the middle of East End news, gossip, celebrations, hopes and fears, troubles and tragedies." His rise to political power was an inevitable Irish process. He knew how to listen, keep a secret, show sympathy, and lend a helping hand. "Often he passed the word on to somebody that so-and-so needed this or that and P. J. Kennedy would appreciate it, asking nothing in return but good will," she writes. Though elected to the Massachusetts House of Representatives and the state Senate, "P.J." "preferred to work quietly, behind the scenes" from his base of political power in East Boston.[20]

In the earlier decades of Irish mass migration, the saloon even functioned as a political meeting place. During the 1830's in New York's rambunctious Sixth Ward (known as the "bloody ould Sixth"), "Dooley's Long-Room was as famed in politics as was ever Tammany Hall," according to a nineteenth-century account. "To hold a meeting there made it

orthodox and regular. The ticket that was indorsed at that
famed political head-quarters carried the ward." So it was on
one evening that a candidate received the endorsement when
his supporters "arrived just in the nick of time to save the
chairman from going out of the window, and the secretary
following him." Instead the opposition chairman and his
followers went out the same window.[21]

The Irish looked to their political leaders to be gregarious
and generous as well as tough. They had to be at home in the
saloons and able to stay in touch with the people. As Al Smith
recalled in his autobiography, the politicians had "very little
spare time to themselves in the summer" since they were
expected to keep up with a steady schedule of outings—their
own and those of other political leaders. Of these annual
summer outings or "political chowders," the one given by "Big
Tim" Sullivan, the political boss of New York's Lower East
Side, was considered the biggest of all. Smith's description
depicted the Irish-American version of "bread and circus."

The outing began with a parade through the Lower East
Side, led by "Big Tim" himself and ending up at the dock
where everyone boarded the old steamer *Grand Republic*. As
many as six thousand people piled onto a boat built to hold
3,500 for the trip to Donnelly's Pavilion on College Point,
Long Island. As soon as the boat landed, everyone headed
straight for breakfast. "Six or seven thousand people could be
seated at a single time. When the head waiter rang a large bell,
waiters would appear on all sides with clam fritters, ham and
eggs, fried potatoes, rolls and coffee."

All day long there were games—fat man's races, hurdle
races, obstacle races, three or four different games of baseball,
with kegs of beer flowing continuously. In the evening, dinner
was served, consisting of clam chowder, roast beef, lamb
chops, ice cream, and coffee. "Returning home at night,"
Smith recalled, "the picnickers would again parade through
the district, and there was great rivalry in the various parts of

the district as to which would give them the greatest reception. Fireworks were so freely used that on the morning after one of the chowders I found my best suit and my straw hat covered with burns from stray sparks." [22]

For an Irish politician like "Big Tim" Sullivan, the response to social legislation came from the gut, not from theory. He supported women's suffrage out of grateful memory to a schoolteacher who bought him a pair of shoes when he was a slum child. He remembered his own sister and mother—"poor and struggling"—and saved a New York State bill establishing a maximum 54-hour week for working women. Frances Perkins, later U.S. Secretary of Labor under Franklin Delano Roosevelt, recalled that she was lobbying for the bill in Albany and it seemed sure of passage. So State Senator Sullivan left for New York, only to be called back when the bill unexpectedly ran into trouble. He came puffing up the hill after being pulled off the Albany boat and assured her: "It's all right, me gal, we are wid ya. De bosses thought they was going to kill your bill, but they forgot about Tim Sullivan. I'm a poor man meself. Me father and me mother were poor and struggling. I see me sister go out to work when she was only fourteen and I know we ought to help these gals by giving 'em a law which will prevent 'em from being broken down while they're still young."

Perkins recalled it as "a simple emotional response with no sophisticated political consideration involved," noting that Sullivan never realized how much nationwide support this would bring to Roosevelt 20 years later.[23] As Wittke summed Sullivan up: "Crooked, loyal, generous, he typified the old-fashioned Irish boss." [24] When he was struck and killed by a train in 1913, 25,000 people attended his funeral.

In responding personally, the political bosses also responded pragmatically, instinctively grasping the uses of power in the expanding cities of a free-wheeling economy in a country whose business was business. They viewed politics as a business, too, and the political machine as the equivalent of a business corporation. It provided continuity in government. Candidates and office-holders came and went, but The Boss remained. When Steffens, in chronicling the empires of big-city bosses, turned to Tammany's Croker, he was instructed on why political bosses were needed: "It's because there's a mayor and a council and judges and—a hundred other men to deal with. A government is nothing but a business, and you can't do business with a lot of officials, who check and cross one another and who come and go, there this year, out the next. A business man wants to do business with one man, and one who is always there to remember and carry out the—business." When Steffens reacted by saying business has no bosses, he was struck by Croker's put-down: "You tell me you have been a Wall Street reporter. If that is true, then you know as well as I do that Wall Street has its bosses just like Tammany and just like the Republican machine." To Steffens, Croker "had morality. He was true to his professional ethics." [25]

In their drive toward power—taking command of their own lives and those of others—the political bosses were successful versions of the struggles of everyday Irish-Americans. The bosses stayed within the mainstream of Irish-American life. They made money by owning saloons and a few gained fame by becoming prizefighters. To sum up the way Irish newcomers "made it" in American politics, John ("Old Smoke") Morrissey can be introduced as a case in point.

As much as any Irish immigrant, Morrissey personified the uphill fight. From a wallpaper factory in Troy, New York, to U.S. Congressman, John Morrissey toiled, fought, politicked, profited, and gambled, winning and losing several fortunes. Born in Tipperary, Morrissey had come over at the age of three with his father, a day laborer. He went to work at the age of twelve and grew up in the harsh world of factory hands and river men. At 17, he was a bouncer in a Troy saloon, later a deck hand on a Hudson River boat, and then one of the runners who victimized immigrants in New York City. Worldly wise as he was, Morrissey did not learn to read and write until he taught himself at the age of 19. Along the way, he earned his nickname, "Old Smoke," during a barroom brawl: after landing on some burning coals from a stove that had been knocked over, he got up with his coattails smoking and flattened his opponent.

Next, Morrissey caught the same "California fever of 1849" that afflicted other Irishmen and bummed cross-country to seek his fortune. He ended up as a prizefighter in the bare-knuckles era that was dominated by fighting Irishmen. In 1853, at the age of 22, Morrissey—who had been described in Troy as a great "broth of a bhoy" and who would win fame as the Irish Strong Boy long before John L. Sullivan—took on "Yankee" Sullivan, a Liverpool Irishman, for the championship. At Boston Four Corners, where New York, Connecticut, and Massachusetts meet, they fought for 37 bruising, bloody rounds before Morrissey won the heavyweight championship. In another celebrated bout in 1858, Morrissey successfully defended his title against a fellow Irishman from Troy, John Carmel Heenan. Then Morrissey retired from the ring, turning over the title to Heenan, who maintained the Irish boxing preeminence and became a national idol.

The next rounds for Morrissey involved the operation of a saloon, establishment of the race track at Saratoga Springs, New York, and of America's first fashionable gambling salon, and prominence in rough-and-tumble New York politics. When Tammany Hall nominated him for Congress in 1866, it drew horror and editorial outrage. The *New York Tribune* editorialized that "public decency and the dignity of the National Legislature have seldom been so boldly outraged," adding that it was "disgraceful enough" to select an ex-prizefighter, but this was also someone who would "owe his nomination to the faro bank." [26] Nonetheless, Morrissey was elected to two terms in Congress and when he died, it was front-page news in the *New York Times*:

> Saratoga, May 1—John Morrissey died at 7:30 o'clock this evening. He had seemed quiet and without any unfavorable symptoms until a little after 5 o'clock. When the New York newspapers were brought in, after 3 o'clock, he motioned for his glass and proceeded to read one. About 5:30 an unfavorable change occurred, and he sank rapidly afterward. Father McMenomy, the Roman Catholic priest, was sent for, and he administered Extreme Unction. Although Mr. Morrissey was failing perceptibly all the time, he appeared conscious until the last. His wife and several servants were present at his death. He died clasping the hand of the priest.[27]

When Morrissey was buried in the city of his obscure beginnings, the funeral, as reported by the *New York Times*, symbolized the promise and glory of politics for Irish-Americans. "Troy never saw such a funeral," the *Times* man reported. . . . "no burial ever evoked so many expressions of sorrow from the mass of the people—the hard, rough workingmen and women in the class out of which Morrissey sprang, and which he always claimed as his, for sympathy and support. They turned out en masse today in their working clothes, and with the grit upon their faces, to watch with tears in their eyes the passage of the funeral procession." The political elite of New York state were also there—lieutenant governor, attorney-general, state senators and assemblymen. The crowd "filled the church to suffocation" and heard "a glowing eulogy of Morrissey as a man and a citizen." After the congregation had passed by for a last look, the coffin was carried to the hearse and, as the body of the poor boy from Tipperary was taken to St. Peter's Cemetery, 15,000 persons watched a grand and somber procession of 50 carriages.[28]

VIII

Patriotic Green

FOR THE IRISH, the Civil War became a proclamation of
their Americanization. They responded to the call to arms in
highly visible numbers, self-consciously waved their green flag
along with the Stars and Stripes, and won general acclaim on
the battlefield. Reflecting the changing image of the Irish, a
war correspondent reported that the Irish 69th Regiment—
"strolling, drunken vagabonds . . . picked up in the low
groggeries of New York"—"fought like tigers" in the first
Battle of Bull Run.[1]

During the Civil War, the Irish moved toward the kind of
acceptance proclaimed after Bull Run by their hero, Thomas
Francis Meagher. Coming to Boston in September, 1861, to
recruit volunteers for the Irish Brigade, Meagher, with the
governor of Massachusetts at his side, told a large crowd in the
city that had so despised the Irish: "Here at this hour I
proclaim it . . . Know-Nothingism is dead. This war, if it

brought no other excellent and salutary fruits, brought with it
this result, that the Irish soldier will henceforth take his stand
proudly by the side of the native-born, and will not fear to look
him straight and sternly in the face, and tell him that he has
been equal to him in his allegiance to the Constitution. This,
too, I know—that every Irishman this side of Mason and
Dixon's line is with me. If there is one who is not, let him take
the next Galway steamer and go home." [2]

The outbreak of the war sparked the Irish to rally 'round the
flag and the cause of saving the Union. Whereas the issue of
slavery left them cold, if not hostile, toward abolitionists,
whom they considered dangerous radicals, the threat to
national unity aroused them. The Boston Pilot summed up the
Irish reaction in the North: "The Union—It Must Be Pre-
served! The Pilot Knows No North, No South." [3]

The Irish viewpoint was articulated by Captain David P.
Conyngham, who distinguished himself in the Irish Brigade.
"The Irish felt that not only was the safety of the great
Republic, the home of their exiled race, at stake, but also, that
the great principles of democracy were at issue with the
aristocratic doctrines of monarchism," he wrote. "The Irish
soldier did not ask whether the colored race were better off as
bondsmen or freemen, he was not going to fight for an abstract
idea." [4] To the Irish, while abolitionism was another example
of the perilous Protestant moralizing that threatened to tear
the country apart, secession was a heresy to be put down.

When the South actually took up arms, Archbishop Hughes
spoke out loudly in favor of supporting the Union. As to
fighting to end slavery, Hughes was characteristically em-
phatic: "We despise, in the name of all Catholics, the 'Idea' of
making this war subservient to the philanthropic nonsense of
abolitionism." [5]

After Fort Sumter was attacked, the Irish lined up to
volunteer. Officially, the U.S. Sanitary Commission reported in
1869 that 144,221 Irish-born soldiers and officers served on the

Union side, a manpower contribution larger than their proportion of the population. Estimates run higher, to 170,000 Irish
soldiers, and a case has even been made for 300,000, based on
casualty figures. Of the Irish-born soldiers officially recorded,
New York had by far the largest number with 51,206. Next
came Pennsylvania (17,418), Illinois (12,041), Massachusetts
(10,007), Ohio (8,129), Missouri (4,362), and Wisconsin (3,621).

In New York, 6,000 immediately volunteered for the 1,000
places in the "Fighting 69th" and the Irish regiment was on its
way by April 23, 1861—only 11 days after the firing on
Sumter. When the regiment marched through the streets of
New York, en route to the steamer that would carry them to
the defense of Washington, huge crowds of Irishmen cheered
and Irish women waved their handkerchiefs. The regiment was
escorted by Irish societies, several fire companies, and units of
Irish police.

As recalled by Michael Cavanagh, a militant Irish nationalist
and "enthusiastic admirer" of Thomas Meagher, the scene
reached a high emotional pitch, "observable in the pale or
flushed faces, the quivering, compressed lips, and misty eyes of
rough, horny-handed toilers, who, commiseratingly, looked on
in respectful though silent sympathy; and in the unrestrained
tears and audible wailings of the maids and matrons who
constituted half, at least, of the dense and ever increasing
crowd that surged and swayed about their armed countrymen. . . ."

Cavanagh also linked the outpouring of emotion to the Irish
dream of eventually fighting the British. There were even
hopes that Great Britain's sympathies for the Southern cause
might lead to war against them. In Cavanagh's recollections of
the 69th's departure day as set down in his 1892 *Memoirs* of
Meagher, "the sentiment which found most frequent expression from old and young, was *not* that of sorrow or regret that
their countrymen were going to battle—but that they were *not*
going to battle on another field" (against Britain).[6]

The Civil War publicly transformed the Irish emotionalism, bravado, and militancy that had once brought nativist sneers. These traits became patriotic fare, even in chilly New England, where recruiting ads urged: "You have fought nobly for the Harp and Shamrock. Fight now for the Stars and Stripes. . . . Your adopted country wants you." [7]

At the first Battle of Bull Run in July, 1861, the scene of Union disaster, the 69th was commanded by Colonel Michael Corcoran, who had won the hearts of his countrymen the year before, and lost his post as commander as a result, by refusing to take part in a parade honoring the visiting Prince of Wales. Corcoran was reinstated when war broke out, and Captain Thomas Meagher, himself an exiled Irish revolutionary, was appointed as his aide.

At a crucial moment in the Battle of Bull Run, after two waves of Union attackers had been devastated by Confederate fire, General William Tecumseh Sherman turned and called to his Irish unit. Sherman's biographer, Lloyd Lewis, has described it as "a medieval moment. . . . long lines of men on scarlet knees in green grass . . . a strange green banner above them . . . bayonets glittering like spears about their bowed heads . . . Latin words rolling from the lips of Father O'Reilly, who commended every soul to God. The benediction done, the men put on their caps, and as they rose, Captain Meagher, standing in front, ran his eye up and down the line and then in fond challenge cried, 'Come on, boys, you've got your chance at last!' " [8]

Like other American battlefield quotes—whether at Bunker Hill or Bastogne—this one had a symbolic quality. The Irish were getting a bloody chance at Americanization. The fighting armies of the North became a melting pot as the battlefield made immigrant and native-born brothers in arms. Close contact and a common enemy changed hostility to acceptance, even understanding. One Boston volunteer, who found the

Irish celebration of St. Patrick's Day strange one year, joined in the next. A visiting Englishman commented that you could not go through a Union camp and say, "There is the sedate Yankee—there the rollicking Irishman." He found that "all seem subdued together into the same good behaviour." [9] On the battlefield, there were no nativists, just men united in danger and a common cause.

Toward the end of the war, an Irish color bearer named Mike Scannel summed up the process when, outdistancing his 19th Massachusetts Regiment near Petersburg, Virginia, he found himself engulfed by a Confederate thrust.

"Hand over those colors, Yankee," a Confederate soldier ordered, pointing a pistol at him.

"Yankee is it, now," said Mike as he handed over the colors, "Faith I've been twenty years in this country and nobody ever paid me the compliment before." [10]

As would be the case in subsequent wars, whether at San Juan Hill or in the Argonne Forest, the Irish kept their identity, while also demonstrating their patriotism. In the Civil War that identity was clearly displayed on the battlefield, as when "ten little drummers fluttered their sticks" after General Sherman ordered the Irish 69th to mount its charge on a boiling afternoon at Bull Run. The men were down to their shirtsleeves and carried nothing but their guns and ammunition. Some had even taken off their shoes.

Rushing over sloping ground where clumps of trees concealed Confederate riflemen, the Irish soldiers charged toward a hill occupied by enemy artillery. They let loose "a loud battle shout, half-English and half-Gaelic"—a sound that would become as distinctive as the Rebel yell.[11] In three hopeless attacks against the entrenched Southern firepower, they charged, fell back, charged again, fell back and tried one more desperate time. In the battle, which ended in a Union rout, the Regiment lost one out of six men, wounded, killed or missing.

A Confederate officer conceded that they held their ground "like a rock in the whirlpool rushing past them. . . . The Irish fought like heroes." [12]

The green flag was their rallying point. At Bull Run, Colonel Corcoran ordered the color bearer to lower the green flag which had become a conspicuous target for enemy riflemen. The soldier protested that he would never lower it, only to be killed an instant later. Another soldier sprang forward to raise the flag and he, too, was killed. A color bearer in Meagher's company named John Keefe had the green banner torn from his hands by a Confederate soldier. He shot him, recapturing the flag and seizing a Confederate one as well. Before he could obey the order to fall back, however, he was overpowered by a squad of rebel soldiers. He went down kicking and fighting. Taken prisoner, Keefe promptly killed his two guards with a revolver concealed in his shirt. He took back the green flag and returned to Union lines, bursting from the thicket and waving the banner to the cheers of his fellow Irishmen.

When their 90-day enlistment period ended, the members of the 69th were mustered out. However, many of them soon rejoined when their dream of a brigade of their own was realized. Meagher, then a colonel, was authorized to form the Irish Brigade, which was initially composed of the 69th, the 88th, and the 63rd New York Volunteers and which set out to join the Union army in Virginia with the symbols of Erin on its green banners. An Irish harp was embroidered in the center, with a sunburst above and a wreath of shamrocks beneath. Their motto, in Gaelic on a crimson scroll, announced: "They shall never retreat from the charge of lances."

All the Irish units proclaimed their identity. The regimental flag of the Massachusetts 28th displayed a harp and a slogan in Gaelic, "Clear the Road." The "Irish Ninth" in Massachusetts carried the inscription, "As allies and strangers thou didst us befriend. As sons and true patriots we do thee defend." Irish exploits on the battlefield were witnessed, described, and praised throughout the war years, creating a cumulative image of heroism. The reports came back in greatest detail to each state about its own units, but the most famous unit by far was the Irish Brigade. It both epitomized and dramatized Irish-American patriotism.

In its first general engagement, the Irish Brigade confronted rebel forces at Fair Oaks, a railroad station six miles east of Richmond, as Union forces were driving toward the Confederate capital. On May 31, 1862, after two Union attacks had been repulsed, General Edwin ("Old Bull") Sumner rode up to the Irish Brigade. A short distance away, Captain Edward Field of the U.S. Artillery watched Sumner doff his hat, baring his gray locks as he made a short speech, "probably the only one of the old hero's life." He told the Brigade that they were his last hope; if they failed, the battle was lost. "I'll go my stars on you," he said, pointing to his shoulder straps. "I want to see how Irishmen fight, and when you run, I'll run too."

The Brigade responded with "a hearty cheer and moved into the woods with the air of men who were going to stay," Captain Field reported. "A fresh crash showed when they struck the enemy. For a few minutes the fire was deafening, then it began to retire. The yells gave way to long continuous cheers, an aide galloped up to order a section of artillery to follow our advancing line, and the battle of Fair Oaks was won. It was an inspiriting opening of a heroic history, and from that day General Sumner swore by the Irish Brigade." [13]

The following September 17 at Antietam—on the bloodiest single day of the Civil War, with 23,000 dead or wounded on both sides—the Irish Brigade achieved its "crowning glory," Captain Field recorded. As Union forces stopped the Confederate invasion of Maryland and Pennsylvania, the Irish Brigade almost disappeared in a surge of fighting. It forced the enemy back beyond a sunken road, "which had been filled with corpses by an enfilading fire from one of our batteries, and presented the most ghastly spectacle of the war," Field reported. "Using this lane as a breastwork, they held it to the close of the fight, losing not a prisoner, having not one straggler, but at a loss of life that was appalling. One regiment lost nearly fifty per cent, another over thirty. The rebels seemed to have a special spite against the green flag, and five color-bearers were shot down successively in a short time. As the last man fell even these Irishmen hesitated a moment to assume a task synonymous with death. "Big Gleason," Captain of the Sixty-third, six feet seven, sprang forward and snatched it up. In a few minutes a bullet struck the staff, shattering it to pieces; Gleason tore the flag from the broken staff, wrapped it around his body, putting his sword-belt over it, and went through the rest of that fight untouched." [14]

A war correspondent at Antietam described the Brigade's advance, led by Meagher (by then a general), to the brow of a hill where the musketry fighting "was the severest and most deadly ever witnessed before—so acknowledged by veterans in the service." His detailed account went on:

> Men on both sides fell in large numbers every minute, and those who were eye-witnesses of the struggle did not think it possible for a single man to escape. The enemy here, at first, were concealed behind a knoll, so that only their heads were exposed. The brigade advanced up the slope with a cheer, when a most deadly fire was poured in by a second line of the enemy concealed in the Sharpsburg road, which at this place is several feet lower than the surrounding surface, forming a complete rifle-pit, and also from a force partially concealed still further to the rear.
>
> The line of the brigade, in its advance up the hill, was broken in the centre temporarily by an obstruction—the right wing having advanced to keep up with the colors—and fell back a short distance, when General Meagher directed that a rail fence—which the enemy a few minutes before had been fighting behind—should be torn down. His men, in face of a galling fire, obeyed the order, when the whole brigade advanced

to the brow of the hill, cheering as they went, and causing the enemy to fall back to their second line—the Sharpsburg road—which is some three feet lower than the surrounding surface.

In this road were massed a large force of infantry, and here was the most hotly contested point of the day. Each brigade of this division was brought into action at this point, and the struggle was truly terrific for more than four hours—the enemy finally, however, were forced from their position. . . .

The brigade suffered terribly. General Meagher's horse was shot under him, and a bullet passed through his clothes. The Sixty-third Regiment of this brigade, always conspicuous for deeds of daring in battle, was particularly so in the battle of Antietam. The colors were shot down sixteen times, and on each occasion a man was ready to spring forward and place the colors in front. John Hartigan, a member of Company H, and only sixteen years old, went some distance in advance of the regiment with the colors, and waved them defiantly in the face of the enemy. The whole brigade gave a cheer that was heard along the lines for a mile, when it advanced up the rising ground and drove the enemy from a strong position.[15]

In December, 1862, the Irish Brigade was devastated by murderous fire from an impregnable Confederate position on Marye's Heights during the Battle of Fredericksburg. In that blundering Union defeat, the Irish effort won praise even from General Robert E. Lee, who later stated: "Never were men so brave. They ennobled their race by their splendid gallantry on that desperate occasion. Though totally routed, they reaped harvest of glory. Their brilliant, though hopeless, assaults on our lines excited the hearty applause of our officers and soldiers." [16]

On the battlefield, General Meagher aroused his men with a fiery challenge to "fellow exiles of Erin." Never mind, he told them, that their green banners had been shot to pieces; put a sprig of evergreen in their hats and then they would still be fighting for their "adopted land beneath the immortal banner of green." Six times, the Brigade was in the midst of the hopeless charges against Marye's Heights as its five regiments were reduced to 200 men. The war correspondent of the *London Times* reported that "after witnessing the gallantry and devotion exhibited" by Meagher's troops and "viewing the hillsides for acres strewn with their corpses thick as autumnal leaves, the spectator can remember nothing but their desperate courage." He noted that the bodies, which were piled up within 40 yards of the stone wall protecting the rebel soldiers, were "the best evidence of what manner of men they were who pressed on to death with the dauntlessness of a race which was gained glory on a thousand battlefields, and never more richly deserved it than at the foot of Marye's Heights on the 13th day of December, 1862." [17]

There were Irish units on the other side of that wall at Marye's Heights as well, companies from North Carolina and Georgia. Altogether, as many as 40,000 Irishmen served on the Confederate side, some of them recruited abroad and conscripted on landing in New Orleans. Lee described the Irish soldier as fighting "not so much for lucre as through the reckless love of adventure, and, moreover, with a chivalrous devotion to the cause he espouses for the time being." Lee singled out Patrick Cleburne, the outstanding Irish general on the Confederate side, as "a dashing military man" who "was all virtue" and who had "inherited the intrepidity of his race." [18]

The green flags carried by Irish units on both sides left no doubt about the harsh confrontation which turned countrymen into enemies in the New World. Yet, as one Irishman said when asked if it weren't a shameful state of affairs: "Sure it isn't a greater shame for an Irishman to fire on Irish colors than for an American to fire on American colors." [19] The ferocity of such fighting was described in a letter home to Ireland by a County Carlow man living in Philadelphia. He described the mutual slaughter at the first Battle of Bull Run when the

Northern 69th faced a southern Irish regiment. The focus of their fighting was the "poor green flag," which changed hands four times before the 69th carried it off. But the cost in lives was "grievous to every Irishman" for "there was more lives lost over that flag than anny other one object was on the field." [20]

In spite of their exploits on the battlefield, the Irish stained their image on the streets of New York with the draft riots of July, 1863. "This most brutal of all civil upheavals cost a greater number of lives than any other incident of domestic violence in American history," historian Richard Hofstadter has noted.[21] Basically, it was a race riot ignited by a draft lottery which was unfairly organized and which inflamed Irish feelings of oppression. The New York Herald called it "a popular outbreak inspired by a burning sense of wrong." [22]

Coming after two years of war in which Irish regiments had suffered such severe losses, the first drawing showed a majority of Irish names among the 1,200 selected, largely poor workers who could not escape conscription by putting up the required $300 or by paying for a substitute. This provision of the draft aroused class antagonisms, while the Emancipation Proclamation in the preceding fall had focused attention on freedom for the slaves. The Irish saw this as a switch in the emphasis of the war from a fight against secession to a fight for abolition. Racial antipathy, which was already evident among Irish manual workers who feared competition from blacks, was aggravated when blacks were used as strikebreakers in New York against longshoremen and stevedores.

The scenario for the violence was thereby established. Fighting began on Monday, July 13, when the police tried to disperse crowds of disgruntled, milling Irish workers who had stayed away from their jobs following publication of the draft lottery names. The draft headquarters was the first target, then the homes of the wealthy, followed by the main target: New York City blacks. The Colored Orphans Asylum, which housed

200 children aged two to 12, was destroyed; all over the city blacks were driven panic-stricken into the streets, burned, stomped, clubbed, hanged, shot. At one point, the police chief, John Kennedy, was almost beaten to death while leading his men, many of them Irish. For three days, the city was terrorized by mobs, only subsiding on the fourth day as Archbishop Hughes addressed a large crowd from his balcony. He pleaded for order and urged his listeners to be peaceable, so that if they "should meet a police officer or a military man, why, just look at him." [23]

There were other draft riots in several Northern cities, but none like New York's. When casualties were estimated, it was clear that the Irish had exhibited here the same ferocity they had shown on the battlefield. Estimates of dead and wounded ranged as high as 1,200, with the actual number at least 300, possibly much higher.[24] Yet, as *Harper's Weekly* noted, Irishmen helped rescue the children from the orphanage; in some neighborhoods, the Irish joined hands to help maintain law and order; the clergy struggled to keep the peace; a large number of the police who fought the mob were themselves Irish.[25] William Shannon has commented that "it was a classic example of the poor in their misery venting their fury on other poor who were even worse off," and "it is one of the ironies of American Irish history that the draft riots in New York occurred only one week after the Irish in the Union Army had played a heroic role in the decisive battle of the War"— Gettysburg on July 3–4.[26]

Overall, what stood out in the aftermath of the Civil War was Irish participation in saving the Union. Northern armies had brought together native-born and immigrants in a way they had never experienced in the cities. Over 400,000 foreign-born fought to save the Union. National consciousness was increased in a nation not even 100 years old, as immigrants—particularly the Irish and the Germans—reached a higher level of participation in the United States.

The press glamourized the Irish, particularly by transform-
ing the phrase "fighting Irish," which had once signified rioting
rowdyism. It became capitalized: "Fighting Irish" was now a
compliment, conjuring up heroism in time of war and heroics
on playing fields. One small touch at San Juan Hill during the
Spanish-American War demonstrated the journalistic reflex.
War correspondents raced around looking for the first soldier
to reach the blockhouse on San Juan Hill, certain that he
would be a "red-haired Irishman." According to Thomas Beer,
they were "warmly disappointed when he proved an ordinary
American of German ancestry." Nineteen years later, another
group of correspondents in World War I "went hunting a
red-haired Irishman who fired the first shot of the American
Expeditionary Force in France." [27]

During World War I, the "Fighting 69th" captured the
spotlight with its famed chaplain, Francis Patrick Duffy, and
its acclaimed commander, William J. ("Wild Bill") Donovan.
Though redesignated the 165th Infantry, the regiment never
lost its celebrated identity as the "Fighting Irish" of the Old
69th. When Father Duffy described the volunteers who sprang
forward to join the unit, he showed how far the Irish image
had progressed. It was not only Irish-Americans who were
proud of their identity. Duffy wrote in his diary: "Ours was a
picked lot. They came mainly from the Irish County Societies
and from the Catholic Athletic Clubs. A number of these latter
Irish bore distinctly German, French, Italian, or Polish names.
They were Irish by adoption, Irish by association or Irish by
conviction." [28]

Among those who were Irish by conviction (and Catholic by
conversion) was the poet Joyce Kilmer who told a reporter that
he belonged in the 69th because he was "half-Irish" (thereby
downplaying his English and Scotch origins). Chaplain Duffy
welcomed him as a regimental historian who would confer
"the gift of immortality" upon the 69th. Kilmer wrote home
enthusiastically that the people he liked best in the regiment

were "the wild Irish." He learned their songs and he agitated to leave his desk job in intelligence to join them at the front. Kilmer did become a battlefield sergeant and then volunteered to replace Donovan's adjutant who had been killed at the front. In that role, he too was killed while on an observation mission with "Wild Bill." Kilmer "was one of those soldiers who had a romantic love of death in battle," Chaplain Duffy noted.[29]

In New York, Kilmer had gone personally to Duffy to ask for transfer to the Old 69th. The regiment was sending its machine-gun trucks around the city with the placard, "Don't join the 69th unless you want to be among the first to go to France." The appeal worked; in the later weeks of its formation, the regiment was turning away 300 volunteers a week and referring them to other units. The promise on the placard was fulfilled; the regiment was selected from all of New York's National Guard regiments to represent the state in the newly-formed 42nd Rainbow Division, being prepared as one of the first units to fight in France with the American Expeditionary Force.

And fight they did. The men of the 69th faced enemy fire for an impressive 180 days. They gained 55 kilometers. They were headquartered in 85 different places. In the fighting 644 men were killed and 2,857 were wounded (some more than once)—thus they went overseas with 3,500 men and suffered 3,501 casualties.

When the regiment marched from its armory to the dock where two troop ships waited to carry them to France, an elderly woman burst through the crowds. She "was crying and laughing at the same time," Kilmer wrote in his unfinished regimental history, as she "thrust into the hands of a bandsman a green flag marked in gold with the Irish harp and the motto 'Erin Go Bragh!' " [30] The old woman's flag went over the top with the regiment in every one of their battles in France.

When the regiment returned to march triumphantly up

New York's Fifth Avenue on April 28, 1919, its members heard for the first time the music for Kilmer's poem, "When the 69th Comes Back," as composed for the occasion by Victor Herbert of light-opera fame (also president of the Friendly Sons of Ireland and of the Friends of Irish Freedom). The regiment carried three flags, the Stars and Stripes, the regimental standard, and a third flag—"a little green flag of Ireland, with harp and motto 'Erin Go Bragh!' which fluttered from a private's bayonet." [31]

IX

American "Irishism"

In the *Irish-American Almanac* for 1875, T. D. Sullivan set
to rhyme the feelings of "The Irish-American":

> Columbia the free is the land of my birth
> And my paths have been all on American earth
> But my blood is as Irish as any can be,
> And my heart is with Erin afar o'er the sea.[1]

This pervasive sentiment in the 19th and early 20th
centuries created a specifically American version of "Irishism."
Just as they came to be regarded as more Catholic than the
Pope, Irish-Americans could be more "Irish" than those in the
old country. The greening of their American identity produced, in extreme form, the stereotypical professional Irishman. Succeeding generations of immigrants remained Irish in
an American sort of way or, rather, became American in an
emphatically Irish way.

The ingredients of that American "Irishism" were constantly set down in rhetoric and rhyme, on formal occasions
and in saloon conversation. Among countless examples, a
Boston Pilot editorial provided a characteristic summary on the
Fourth of July, 1874. "Though American by nationality, we are
yet Irish by race," the *Pilot* stated. "Ireland is our fatherland,
and the Irish people over the world are our blood relations.
And this relationship shall exist between our children and their
children. The patron saint of Ireland is also the patron saint of
the Irish race throughout the globe. The historic glories of the
Emerald Isle are common property of the race; the persecu-
tions inflicted on it—the shame and the contumely heaped
upon it—have alike been our misfortune. We owe a duty to
Ireland. Ireland looks to us in this Great Republic of the West
for deliverance: to deny that we owe this duty . . . would be
to proclaim to mankind our own baseness and degeneracy."

Irishism was above all militant, as was demonstrated in the
various ways Irish-Americans proclaimed their identity. They
formed myriad organizations—social clubs, militia companies,
firefighting brigades, literary groups, charitable societies. They
delighted in donning uniforms and marching up Main Street.
They relished outings with their own kind, and while they
loved a peaceful parade, they were ready to riot when feeling
oppressed or wronged. They even formed a quasi-state of their
own and set up a capitol on New York's Union Square.

The Irish and the English had always shared a strange,
twisted relationship that seemed to unhinge both sides. Cecil
Woodham-Smith, writing from an English historian's viewpoint, comments that the English behaved in Ireland in a
completely uncharacteristic way: "as a nation, the English
have proved themselves capable of generosity, tolerance and
magnanimity, but not where Ireland is concerned." She quotes
the writer and wit, Sydney Smith: "The moment the very
name of Ireland is mentioned, the English seem to bid adieu to
common feeling, common prudence, and common sense, and

to act with the barbarity of tyrants and the fatuity of idiots." [2]

Bringing to the New World the feelings of oppression engendered by their experience with the English, the Irish found a free arena in which they could talk and act out their love-hate feelings. Irish-Americans developed a pronounced style of fighting back. Their symbols evoked militant feelings: "Wearing of the Green," harp, phoenix, wolfhound, sunburst, shamrock, Gaelic slogans. Historical events became emotional landmarks, particularly the Famine Years and the July 12 anniversary of the 1690 Battle of Boyne in which William III of England established Protestant ascendancy in the British Isles (Protestant Orangemen take their name and their inflammatory color from the King's family). All this was commingled with the names of Irish heroes, invoked as if they had magical powers. So it was that the Irish as Americans lived in a highly-charged emotional context, filled with melodramatic anniversaries, names, and symbols that revolved around the twin poles of love for Ireland and hate for England.

In post-Civil War America, Maguire found everywhere among the Irish "the same feeling of passionate love, the same feeling of passionate hate." An Irish captain from the Civil War visited him and insisted on showing his wounds—a bullet hole in the neck, a scar near his spine, a shattered arm, assorted minor scars. Then, "his eyes sparkled, and his face became suffused with enthusiasm, as, suddenly flinging aloft his other arm, lean and sinewy, he exclaimed in a voice of concentrated passion—'This is the only arm I have left, and, so help me God! I'd give it and every drop of my heart's blood, if I could only strike one blow for Ireland. I'd be satisfied to die of my wounds then, for I'd die happy in her cause.'"

In the depths of an Illinois mine, Maguire sat in a dark, murky passageway where he was "harangued in fiery accents" on British iniquities by a young miner who knew the story of Irish nationalism by heart. An Irish foreman listened with "a deep murmur of satisfaction," uttering, "Thrue of you, boy!"

as the miner cited events and persons. The foreman added that "he'd give his life if necessary, and gladly too, for the country that he was ever thinking of, and that was dear to his heart." [3]

Another visitor, touring North America in 1857–1858, was taken aback by a confrontation in the bar at Willard's Hotel in Washington where some U.S. Congressmen were extolling British heroism against Indian mutineers. A nearby Irishman with a heavy brogue "burst in upon us with a volley of oaths so awful and so disgusting that no gentleman or man of common decency would whisper them, much more print them, and imprecated such wrath of heaven upon England and upon Englishmen in India and at home, that I fairly lost breath in the excess of my surprise at hearing such abominable sentiments in the mouth of a human being." The visitor, being informed that the angry Irishman was well-known and much respected, noted that, though he was "much more violent" than the Irish generally, the feeling was "only too common among men of his race" who "brought their passions and their prejudices into the great arena of American politics." [4]

Growing up in the 1890's as a second-generation Irish-American, Elizabeth Gurley ("Ma") Flynn, who became a leading American Communist, remembered that "as children, we drew in a burning hatred of British rule with our mother's milk." In her autobiography, she proudly reported that her forefathers took part in every uprising against the British. (Another leading American Communist, William Z. Foster, was also a child of English-hating Irish immmigrants.) "Until my father died, at over eighty, he never said *England* without adding, 'God damn her!,' " Flynn recalled. "Before I was ten I knew of the great heroes—Robert Emmet, Wolfe Tone, Michael Davitt, Parnell, and O'Donovan Rossa, who was chained hand and foot, like a dog, and had to eat from a tin plate on the floor of a British prison." [5]

Irish-Americans nurtured both fantasies and frustrations. The fantasy bred grandiose, outrageous plans. The frustration erupted in rioting. But always the militancy, always the well-publicized plans, the rhetoric, and the resolutions, begin ning in 1842 with the first national gathering of Irish-Americans on behalf of Ireland. It took place in Philadelphia on Washington's Birthday with 24 delegations from 26 different cities and towns.

Historian George Potter aptly characterizes the meeting as "unique in the Republic." People of a single nationality came together openly from all parts of the country to demand change in a foreign country by invoking American principles. They demanded that England repeal its 1800 Act of Union which had abolished the independent Irish Parliament and merged England and Ireland. In the end, after angry bickering over resolutions, the convention ended with anti-English speeches and three cheers for Ireland, the Irish leader Daniel O'Connel, Repeal, Philadelphia, and the ladies. The *Boston Pilot* would subsequently call the convention a "miserable abortion." [6]

Given the mightiness of Ireland's enemy—Great Britain— and the staggering mismatch, the feelings of Irish-Americans needed outlets. If they were given to gestures weighted down with rhetoric and if the word outraced the deed, no matter. Their feelings cried out for release. Thus, they influenced the progress of nationalism in Ireland and shaped their Irish-American identity.

A characteristic example was the refusal of Colonel Michael Corcoran to lead his 69th Regiment in a New York parade honoring the visit of Britain's Prince of Wales in the fall of 1860. Corcoran became a hero among Irish-Americans and lost his command (which, as noted earlier, was restored when the Civil War began). More than three years later, on January 22, 1864, that gesture of defiance against the "beardless youth" was recalled in a memorial evening for Corcoran, who died during the Civil War. The audience, cited as the largest in the history of New York's Cooper Institute Hall, heard General

Thomas Meagher praise Corcoran. As he spoke, there was a bust of Corcoran on the stage, flanked on each side by a uniformed youngster, one holding an American flag, the other an Irish flag. Meagher told the cheering crowd that Corcoran had "refused lawfully as a citizen, courageously as a soldier, indignantly as an Irishman (cheers); refused to parade his stalwart regiment in honor of the beardless youth, who, succeeding to the spoils of the Tudors and Stuarts was destined one day to wield the sceptre that had been the scourge of Ireland. . . ." [7]

Among those sitting in places of honor at Cooper Hall were Civil War veterans of the 69th Regiment and leaders of the Fenians, the American counterpart of the Irish Revolutionary brotherhood. The two strands of "Fighting Irish" were closely linked; New York militia companies were the U.S. center for Irish revolutionary movements and many Irishmen joined the Civil War army with an eye to fighting England another day. They welcomed the military training and experience. Fenians, who had organized in 1858 to free Ireland, were identifiable elements in the Union army and they came out of the Civil War eager to fight for their cause.

A Civil War episode that illustrated their emotional bonding occurred when two former members of the Fenian's Phoenix Brigade fell in action with the 37th New York Volunteers ("Irish Rifles") at Williamsburg, Virginia, in May, 1862. Lieutenants Patrick H. Hayes and Jeremiah O'Leary "sleep together on the field where they fell," a fellow Fenian reported. "Their faithful Fenian Brothers dug their grave at the foot of an oak tree, and laid them, tenderly and lovingly, side by side, their arms twined around each other's neck— covered them with the greenest of shamrocked sods, and, with fervent prayers for their soul's repose—left them to await a happy resurrection." [8]

The "Fenian Marseillaise" set forth the spirit and the intention of that most militant branch of the militant Irish:

> Away with speech, and brother, reach me down
>   that rifle gun.
> By her sweet voice, and hers alone, the rights
>   of man are won.
> Fling down the pen; when heroic men pine sad in
>   dungeons alone,
> 'Tis bayonets bright with good red blood, should
>   plead before the throne.[9]

The Fenian movement sprang from the ongoing support for Irish independence, expressed in money collected for Irish nationalist leaders, and in organizations like New York's "Irishman's Universal Civil and Military Republican Union" (formed in 1854 to free Ireland) and the Massachusetts Emigrant Aid Society (formed in 1855 to finance the return of immigrants as freedom fighters). Renamed the American-Irish Aid Society, the latter organization held a New York convention of delegates from 24 states in 1855, but soon withered away. It was succeeded by the Emmet Monument Association, which in turn led to the organization named after an ancient warrior band from Irish mythology, the Fenians. It was the Fenians who organized their own quasi-state.

In Ireland, the Irish Revolutionary Brotherhood followed the traditional European blueprint for revolutionaries, organizing in secret cells. In the United States, its Fenian counterpart was thoroughly Americanized, from holding an 1865 convention in Philadelphia to drafting a constitution providing for a president and a congress. The modeling was obvious, as was the flagrancy of the militant style. At the Fenian's New York City capitol in a Union Square mansion, the Fenian flag of harp and sunburst flew boldly.

The Fenians also selected a Secretary of War, General T. W. Sweeny, a hero of the Mexican War and a Civil War infantry commander, and thereby moved toward what has been cited as "the most amazing example of group activity by an immigrant element in United States history." [10] A full-scale invasion of Canada was planned, supplanting an even more incredible plan to send an invasion force directly to the British Isles. The Fenians hoped to start a chain reaction that would lead to revolution in Ireland and Canada (if not a swap of a conquered Canada for Ireland), recognition of an Irish republic by the United States, even a war between England and the United States.

It was no private affair. The Canadians had spies reporting on the invasion plans and the English government received regular reports on Fenian movements from an informer. The U.S. government was aware of arms shipments moving to the border, but made no serious effort to stop the Fenians. Reluctant to inflame Irish voters, the U.S. government was itself at odds with England over compensation for her aid to the Confederacy, with some leading Americans suggesting that this include the annexation of Canada.

Meanwhile, the Fenians were talking openly of military actions, holding rallies and picnics, collecting money, and recruiting soldiers and officers (whose uniforms consisted of dark green coats, green sashes, and epaulets with phoenixes, sunbursts, and shamrocks for decoration). At one rally in March, 1866, over 100,000 Irish gathered at the picnic grounds in Jones Woods, in New York's Yorkville section, to cheer on the Fenians. While well-established Irish-Americans shied away from them, mass support for the Fenians came from the working classes that formed the bulk of the Irish-American population.

Fenian Secretary of War Sweeny mapped out an elaborate, three-pronged invasion plan that called for deployment of the main force at Buffalo, New York. The right wing was along the Vermont border, the left wing at Chicago. Fenian units from as far south as Louisiana and as far west as Iowa were ordered to rendezvous points in anticipation of an invasion set for the first week of June, 1866. Lack of transportation and coordination and the belated intervention of the U.S. government—

along with the essential implausibility of the invasion—reduced the plan to nothing more than a flamboyant gesture. It did not help Irish independence as much as it harnessed Irish-American emotions.

The main invasion episode involved the Fenians at Buffalo who were commanded by a dashing Civil War captain, John O'Neill. On the night of May 31, he led a force of about 800, mostly Civil War veterans, across the Niagara River to capture the village of Fort Erie. The Fenians cheered as they raised their flag on British soil; in fact, a number of them spent that first day of June celebrating, leaving them in no shape for further battle.

When O'Neill received reports that two British units were moving to converge at the neck of the peninsula where Fort Erie stands, he rushed to intervene. Digging in at Ridgeway, Canada, O'Neill's men defeated a larger Canadian force at the Battle of Limestone Ridge on June 2. O'Neill decided to return to Fort Erie—which he had to recapture a second time—in order to await reinforcements from the 3,000 Fenian volunteers camped in Buffalo. But the U.S. gunboat *Michigan* prevented either reinforcements or supplies from reaching O'Neill, forcing him to return to the United States. On June 3, the Fenians climbed onto tugboats and headed back to Buffalo, only to be arrested in mid-river by the *Michigan*. The invasion toll was eight Fenians killed and 20 wounded, 12 Canadians killed and 40 wounded.

At St. Albans, Vermont, 1,000 Fenians moved briefly into Canada and occupied hill positions before being forced to turn back. The venture "was a futile gesture," notes William D'Arcy in his study of the Fenian movement, "as the only thing accomplished was the capture of a British flag." [11]

O'Neill tried again in 1870. He set May 24, Queen Victoria's birthday, as the date for two invasions, one from Franklin, Vermont, the other from Malone, New York. Although only a few hundred volunteers had arrived at Franklin, O'Neill led the attack by 200 men, a day late, on the 25th. The Canadian forces were well-prepared and waiting. In the exchange of fire, the Fenians fell back, which enraged O'Neill, who rode to the rear to get reinforcements. He ran straight into the U.S. marshal, who arrested him on the spot and hauled him into his carriage. O'Neill was then driven past his open-mouthed troops to jail in order to face a charge of violating the neutrality laws. At Malone, New York, the Fenian force ventured ever so slightly onto Canadian soil and was immediately driven back.

Fenian volunteers, disgusted with the outcome, deserted by the hundreds; the railroads readily transported them at half fare to get rid of them. Newspapers denounced the invasion as a second Fenian fiasco, with the *New York Times* commenting that even if the Fenians had conquered Canada, "nobody believes it would produce the liberation of Ireland from British rule. It would be just as sensible to expect Russia to liberate Poland if she heard that our Polish fellow-citizens had overpowered the garrisons of Alaska." [12]

The Fenians were outrageous and also well-publicized. The movement made a strong public impact as it was covered extensively by the press. Their gingerly treatment at the hands of the government demonstrated the political impact of the Irish; though the Fenian Brotherhood never included more than 45,000 members, it had much popular support among the Irish. Politicians courted the Fenians and they courted the politicians, even after the movement disintegrated with the second invasion attempt.

The U.S. government itself bowed in their direction with a general pardon signed by President Grant. (On a visit to St. Louis, Grant was handed a petition to free O'Neill with two columns of signatures ten feet long.) Even the English went along by releasing Fenians held in British prisons. When five such Fenians arrived in New York on January 19, 1871, they were lionized, and not only by the Irish. The U.S. Congress passed a resolution, 172 to 21, extending "a cordial welcome to the capital, also to the country." [13]

When the Cunard steamer *Cuba* reached New York harbor, the Republicans and Democrats raced each other to the boat to welcome the Fenians. Thomas Murphy, the city's Republican boss and collector of the port, won the race, bearing greetings from President Grant. Tammany Hall chieftains were right behind. Murphy had elegant rooms reserved at the Astor Hotel, Tammany a sumptuous suite at the Metropolitan Hotel. The reception committees promptly started arguing over the *prize*—five Irish revolutionaries. A public brawl was avoided only when the "Cuba Five" turned down both invitations and stayed on board ship the first night. Then they moved into Sweeny's Hotel, as the city showered them with parades and receptions and Tammany presented a gift of $15,000.

Politicians and government officials had to be careful of Irish sensibilities, so readily translated into votes and, also, into riots. As historian Wittke notes, "almost anything could set off a first-class riot" [14]—election-day disputes and rivalries, interruption of a Catholic service, burning an effigy of St. Patrick on his feast day, evicting an Irishman from a circus tent for refusing to put out his pipe (fellow railroad workers in Somerset, Ohio, joined in that 1853 riot). For six months before and after the arrival of the "Cuba Five," Irish volatility was demonstrated in the infamous Orange Riots in New York City.

The provocation was a parade of Orangemen on July 12, 1870. For the first time in New York, the Orangemen planned a major celebration, beginning with a procession to a picnic, followed by a dance. About 2,500 men, women, and children marched along "in full Orange regalia," playing "Boyne Water," "Derry," and "other tunes obnoxious to the Catholics." The manner in which violence erupted demonstrated how readily the Irish could be aroused. About 200 jeering persons who were following the procession encountered a large number of Irish laborers working on the road and urged them to join in. The laborers immediately stopped work and came along, swelling the crowd to 500. By that time, the Orangemen were enjoying their picnic. When showered with stones, they responded by wielding shovels, clubs, and stones in "a scene of terrific confusion." After the police broke up the fighting, the Irish mob divided into two groups; one returned to attack the Orangemen in the picnic grove and the other went after a large group that had already left the picnic.

Battering down the fence around the park, rioters went after the Orangemen a second time: "A terrible fight followed, and amid the shouts and oaths of the men and screams of women and children, occasional pistol-shots were heard, showing that murder was being done. The enraged, unarmed Orangemen wrenched hand rails from the fence, tore up small trees and seized anything and everything that would serve for a weapon." Finally, police reinforcements broke up this battle.

Police also had to protect the Orangemen, women, and children who had fled for the Eighth Avenue streetcars. The "shouts, oaths, and screams could be heard blocks off." In his account, published shortly after the riot, the popular historian, Joel Tyler Headley, reported that "the most intense excitement prevailed among the Irish population of the city, and it was evident that it needed only a suitable occasion to bring on another conflict." [15]

The following year the Irish Hibernian Society publicly announced that it would disrupt any July 12 parade by Orangemen. When the Protestants asked the police superintendent for protection, he responded by banning the parade because of the threat of violence. As far as the press and the Orangemen in particular were concerned, this was a declaration that the streets of New York belonged to Irish Catholics. The *New York Times* fumed that the city authorities "now officially proclaim that the city is absolutely in the hands of the Irish Catholics." A leading Hibernian called the police superintendent's decision "the greatest concession ever given the Irish." [16]

However, on the day before the scheduled parade, the mayor and the governor reversed the decision and announced that the Orangemen's parade would be protected. A force of 700 policemen and 5,000 militiamen were called out to protect less than 100 Orangemen. At various points in the procession, single shots rang out, until at the corner of Eighth Avenue and Twenty-Fourth Street a single tragic shot caused a line of muskets to be pointed in its direction. Suddenly, without orders, the militiamen let loose a wild burst of fire, creating "a scene of indescribable confusion. . . . Men, women, and children, screaming in wild terror, were fleeing in every direction. . . ." [17] The procession continued through a somber city without further incident but at the cost of 37 civilians killed and 67 wounded. Among the police and militiamen, two were killed and 24 wounded, mainly as the result of gunfire by fellow militiamen.

In a much-discussed article for the *Boston Pilot*, John Boyle O'Reilly addressed himself to the great majority of Irish in America who bore "the blame and the shame" of the 1870 and 1871 Orange riots. He embodied the voice of reason and moderation in the Irish-American community, represented by the large number of Irish policemen who helped to protect the Orangemen and the pleas of the Catholic clergy to keep the peace. "Certain it is that the Orange procession is not a pleasant sight to *any* Irish Catholic, however unprejudiced," he wrote, "but it is just as certain that the Irish Catholics of this country, as a body, condemn all breach of the law in attacking an Orange procession, just as honestly as they would condemn a riot of any other criminal nature." [18] O'Reilly reflected the growing moderation that was evident among the more established Irish-Americans who had not lost their feeling for Ireland but felt uncomfortable with riotous militancy. As a perceptive student of the Irish experience has noted, "mostly the Irish wanted to be middle-class and respectable." [19]

Nonetheless, the Irish image of militancy and violence remained conspicuous, particularly when the underground terrorism of the Molly Maguires in the 1860's and early 1870's was added to the open heroics of the Fenians and the public outbursts of Irish rioters. Operating as a secret faction within local lodges of the Ancient Order of Hibernians, the Molly Maguires terrorized the anthracite coal country of northeastern Pennsylvania. In a scholarly study of Irish-American nationalism, Thomas Brown has compared the Molly Maguires to the Mafia. They were credited with more destruction than they earned through either their organization or their crimes, but their "terror was real enough." [20]

The style of the Molly Maguires was imported from the old country in response to the familiar Irish encounter with oppression. In Pennsylvania, the oppressors were mine owners who brutalized the miners and their families. The miners went down into the dangerous hell of the mines, often with their children along, digging up wealth for the owners and a marginal living for themselves. New waves of immigrants enabled the owners to keep wages low; workers were forced to live in company houses and buy at company stores in between periods of idleness when they earned nothing. Even while working, many a miner received, instead of his monthly pay, a "bobtail check" showing that he owed the company money. When workers tried to organize, the owners intimidated them, and when fledgling labor organizations protested or struck, they were crushed.

As in Ireland, the Irish went underground to fight back. Their targets were the mine operators and bosses, who were mainly Welsh and English—adding ethnic and religious fuel to their hatred. Threatening notices bearing sketches of coffins were sent out, individuals were ambushed and beaten, mine bosses attacked and killed in their homes. (There were nine murders in 1874–1875.) And, of course, no one saw a thing, since the informer was a hated figure and a candidate for murder himself. Moreover, as far as the miners were concerned, the Molly Maguires were fighting for their rights.

The climax was entirely an Irish affair. The mine owners were led by an Irish immigrant named Franklin B. Gowen, who had achieved success as a lawyer, railroad president, and mine operator. James McParlan, the epitome of the swashbuckling, generous, roguish, charming, devil-may-care Irishman from County Armagh, went in as a Pinkerton agent to infiltrate the Molly Maguires. He succeeded so well that—with the help of high-handed legal proceedings—19 Molly Maguires were hanged after much-publicized trials in 1876.

This effectively ended the Molly Maguire episode but dramatized the need for labor to organize, particularly Irish workers who were generally low on the job ladder. Thus, it had been natural for the Irish to rally around the Noble Order of the Knights of Labor when it was founded in 1869 as the first national labor organization. The great early leader of the Knights was Terence Powderly, whose father had left Ireland after a fight with his landlord. Chosen Grand Master Workman in 1879, Powderly led the labor organization out into the open after early years of secrecy as protection against management. By 1886, 800,000 had joined the Knights, a formidable total for those days. Another dimension was added to Irish militancy— Irish workers joined labor organizations in large numbers and produced a tradition of Irish labor leaders.

While the Irish gradually were weaned away from self-centered Irish-American organizations, this happened only as fast as American acceptance and success permitted. Even then, their identity was never abandoned as the Irish went from self-defense to self-assertion to aggressive economic and political demands. Emotionally, too, the Irish, as did all other immigrants, banded together. They enjoyed the warmth of the familiar and the sunshine of ready acceptance, as epitomized in an anonymous rhyme, "What the [County] Armagh Men's Association Means to Me":

> A place where I can spend an evening for less than
> 50 cents
> A little time that takes me back to fond memories
> of my birthplace
> An organization with a human heart
> A right to the free expression of my thoughts
> A friendly debate and a view of the other fellows side
> Warm friends who will give me a hand when I'm down
> A tradition carried on by the Nugent's, McCooey's,
> Byrnes, Callaghan's, Kane's and McCoy's
> A pride in the things that are best in men.[21]

Irish-American organizations also constituted do-it-yourself welfare agencies, particularly to provide illness compensation and death benefits. For example, even in a comparatively small city like Dayton, Ohio, the Irish Catholic Benevolent Union dispensed over $100,000 in charities during its first year, 1869; the Ancient Order of Hibernians, founded in 1836, became a flourishing insurance agency that in 1886 provided $300,000 in sick benefits, burial expenses, and charities. Boston had the Charitable Irish Society as its most prominent example; New York had the Friendly Sons of St. Patrick (its books from 1805 to 1829 contained 70 columns listing names of charity recipients).

These organizations took themselves very seriously; they laid down the law and imposed a sweeping array of fines to keep members in line. The fines of the Hibernian Society of Milwaukee—described as not at all "exceptional" by a student of such societies—levied 50 cents on officers for missing a meeting, 10 cents on ordinary members. Altogether, 13 different types of fines were imposed. Missing a funeral was a $1 fine; attending while drunk cost $1 the first time, $2 the second time. Leaving the room during a meeting without permission carried a fine of 25 cents, and if anyone elected to office refused to serve he was fined $1. The Irish Benevolent Society of Lowell, Massachusetts, was very specific on behavior at meetings: losing one's temper, putting down a fellow member's motives, or casting aspersions on the society meant a 25-cent fine and expulsion from the hall if the offender did not come to order. St. Augustine's Beneficial Society of Philadelphia fined members 25 cents for smoking during a meeting and $1 for playing cards, dice, or any other game during a meeting.[22] Clearly, no rowdy Irish need apply.

While Irish-American organizations gradually lost their wide popular appeal, becoming less necessary both in practical and fraternal terms, they clung to the one day on which they must emerge without fail. Any organization not visible on *that* day truly was dead. On March 17, all the strands of Irish-American life were woven together—piety, politics, and patriotism—all wrapped in green symbols.

Late in the nineteenth century, the *Irish World* expressed itself in the following stanza in response to the question: "How Long Will St. Patrick's Day Live Among Irish-Americans?"

> While in veins of Irish manhood flows one drop of
> Irish blood;
> While in hearts of Ireland's daughters beats
> true Irish womanhood;
> While God sends to Irish mothers babes to
> suckle, boys to rear;
> While God sends to Irish fathers one man child
> thy name to bear.[23]

When John D. Crimmins of New York's Friendly Sons of St. Patrick traced the origins of Irish-American celebrations of March 17, he limited himself to the "more prominent, notable and curious" instances. Still, he drew on the records of 38 different organizations in New York, Massachusetts, Connecticut, Pennsylvania, Rhode Island, Maryland, Virginia, South Carolina, and Georgia for an account of the first 108 years, beginning with the 1737 celebration of Boston's Charitable Irish Society (which was originally Irish Protestant).[24]

After citing the celebrations that took place in colonial America, Crimmins reported that St. Patrick's Day was "enthusiastically observed in the American army during the Revolution." This was the case at Valley Forge in 1778, and the day was singled out by Washington's official order for the 17th of March, 1780, in which he praised the Parliament of Ireland and directed that "all Fatigue and Working Parties cease" for that day.[25]

Throughout the nineteenth century, the Irish celebrated their day with a banquet that grew more elegant and sumptuous as they prospered. In Boston, a two-tier celebration emerged: the elaborate dinner of the Irish Charitable Society and the "bone and sinew" dinner of the Shamrock Society. But a fancy dinner could not handle all the celebrants, nor could all of them afford one. However, a parade, followed by Mass, was another matter. That became the standard public manifestation of "Irishism." Observed one impressed bystander in 1852 after New York's first giant St. Patrick's Day parade: "Why, sure these can't be all Irish; there are not so many in this city, at least!" In the decades immediately preceding the Civil War, the celebrations were taking place from New York to San Francisco, including small cities and towns like Keokuk, Iowa, Alton, Illinois, and Pottsville, Pennsylvania.

At first an assertion of the Irish presence and identity, the day's celebration became a symbol of Irish and, also, Catholic power in America. Everyone cheered, priest and politician, bartender and storekeeper, reporter and neighbor. The day literally "greened" the color of clothes, banners, and buntings. In the parade of 1870, New York's Mayor Oakley Hall did not stop at wearing a shamrock. His tie, kid gloves, and coat were green!

Newspapers added to the rhetoric that accompanied St. Patrick's Day, a day on which praise was showered upon the Irish by themselves and all those around them. On that same St. Patrick's Day in 1870, the *New York Times* welcomed the day with editorial applause characteristic of public accept-ance: "Let us think of the procession and the pageant, of the harp and the sunburst, of the cheerful lads and blushing lasses and of the rich brogue." The St. Patrick's Day parade was "full of hearrt and soul," "all compact of significance and enthusi-asm—an outpouring of genuine rejoicing, a boiling over, in a word, of jovial patriotism and effervescent vitality."

The *New York Times*, as a voice of the American Establish-ment, was praising Irish militancy. The celebration was "a perennial token of Irish nationality as well as of Irish religion—a sign that, although scattered far and wide, Irish-men still hold to their love of country and countrymen, and never forget the verdant home they fondly call the gem of the sea," after coming to "an arena where the strong points of the Irish genius and character have full scope to show the world of what they are capable." [26]

Such responses reflect the success of "Irishism" in America. The Irish converted other Americans—immigrants from all over the world—to the Wearing of the Green. It was a temporary but annual conversion, and an incredible act of recognition for an immigrant group that had been so badly tarred. The Irish not only won acceptance for *their* day, but persuaded everyone else to join in, an achievement matched by no other immigrant group.

As Finley Peter Dunne's "Mr. Dooley" opined early in this century, "But ivrybody is an Irishman on Pathrick's Day. Schwartzmeister comes up wearin' a green cravat an' a yard long green badge an' says: 'Faugh-a-ballagh, Herr Dooley,' which he thinks is Irish f'r 'Good Mornin'.' But ye niver can teach him annything. He's been in this counthry forty years an' don't know th' language. Me good frind Ikey Cohen jines me an' I observe he's left the glassware at home an' is wearin' emeralds in th' front iv his shirt. Like as not along will come little Hip Lung fr'm down th' sthreet with a package iv shirts undhr his ar-arm, an' a green ribbon in his cue." [27]

X

Irish-Americanism

ON NOVEMBER 6, 1910, an Irishman named George F. Mulligan delivered a speech advising the Greek Achaian League of Chicago on how to Americanize. By then, it had come to that; the Irish were models of the Americanization process for incoming immigrants.

Mulligan pointed out to newly-arrived Greek immigrants that they did not see newspapers citing "Mike O'Brien, an Irishman" or "Herman Meyersberger, a German!" But they did read "George Dontopoulos, a Greek," as though Greeks "were some strange and unknown factor in modern civilization." He told them that they had only themselves to blame—"your own disunion, your own lack of organization, lies at the bottom of the public's lack of respect for you."

Learn from the Irish, Mulligan urged the Greeks, band together, organize ("one slender stick" can be broken easily, but not "a hundred sticks bound together tightly") and you

154

"will soon be found in the police department, the fire department, the city council, in city and county offices, in the state legislature, and in Congress." [1] Just like Irish-Americans.

Mulligan's lesson in Americanization had been learned and applied by the Irish. They had responded to the realities confronting immigrants in America. The New World's hospitality could not be taken for granted; a place had to be won in a competitive and hostile arena; America only helped those who helped themselves. In this setting, Irish traits inexorably were metamorphosed into assets. The Irish became adepts of the so-called melting pot.

Their own history had prepared the Irish. Coming from the Old Country where they were landless and powerless, always fighting from a disadvantaged position, the Irish continued fighting in America—but with a difference. Here they could gain power. The timing and the setting of their arrival enabled them to overcome disadvantage by being energetic and organized. America needed people, the cities were booming, and the established American Protestants created at least a partial vacuum by not competing seriously for urban political power.

Whereas in Ireland they were outsiders religiously and politically, the Irish were outsiders socially and economically in America. Taking the roads open to them in politics and in religion, the Irish travelled toward power. They had a headstart chronologically on other foreign groups and could rise as newer immigrants came along to occupy the bottom rungs of American society.

For Protestant Americans, power was the country's "dirty little secret," unsuited to the moralizing posture that they assumed. To the Irish, power was a commodity worth fighting for, and fight they did—as already noted—in the areas of politics, religion, and Irish nationalism. As Irish-American historian Thomas Brown points out, "Nothing strikes the historian of the American Irish so forcibly as their desire to wield power. As churchmen, nationalists, and politicians, they were possessed by the need to bend others to their will." [2]

Other tendencies contributed to Irish-Americanism. Their deeply-ingrained sense of loyalty turned the Irish into superpatriots, suspicious of nonconformists and ready to volunteer for U.S. wars—a frame of mind that suited a jingoistic America. Their preference for the practical and pragmatic in public affairs emphasized the hero as man of action, much in the popularized six-shooter tradition of settling the West. (Even impractical Irish dreamers envisioned great actions taken and great victories won.) Given even a measure of success, the Irish began fitting into the American style. As early as the 1850's, a visiting Englishman wrote that the "Irish may almost be said to be more Americanized than the Americans." [3]

As they succeeded, particularly in politics and religion, the Irish occupied the special role of go-between for newer immigrants. They were not distant models. It was Irish-Americans whom new immigrant groups encountered as the officials at Ellis Island, as the policemen, firemen, city workers, precinct captains, ward chieftains, and machine bosses. To early twentieth-century immigrants, the Irish were the "Americans," for, as rightly pointed out by William Shannon in his study of the Irish, "to a large extent Protestant America abandoned to the Irish the task of politicking, policing, and dealing with the newcomers." [4] To newly-arrived Catholic immigrants from southern and eastern Europe, their church was an Irish church, dominated by the style as well as the power of Irish Catholics.

The Jewish-American humorist Harry Golden has described how an Irish judge "Americanized" his father on the day in 1910 that he took his oath of citizenship. After studying the Declaration of Independence, the Constitution, and the laws of New York State, Golden's father and his fellow immigrants appeared before "a sober, dignified, white-haired Irish judge" and answered questions on American history and the American system. "They raised their right hands and forswore allegiance to Emperor Franz-Joseph and pledged themselves to the American destiny. After the oath, the judge said, 'Now you are all American citizens.' Lowering his voice, he continued, 'And don't forget to vote the straight Democratic ticket.' My father told this story about Tammany for the rest of his life and he always said that he was not only made a citizen that day but completely Americanized." [5]

City police forces were particularly obvious as Irish vestibules to Americanization. Of New York City's 1,149 policemen in 1855, 431 were immigrants, 305 of them Irish. Thirty years later, the Irish proportion of the New York force was almost twice their proportion of the city's population. This pattern included the South, where, as early as the pre-Civil War period, Irish policemen predominated in New Orleans; and it extended to San Francisco where, by the late 1870's, one-third of the force had Irish names. For Irish immigrants who had been victims of the arm of the law, it was a tempting turnabout to become that very arm.

In the process, the Irish made a point of taking care of their own, a pattern that became clear in city governments throughout the country. This was particularly the case in big cities like New York, where the much-quoted sage of Tammany, George Washington Plunkitt, explained why the newly-arrived Irishman is "grateful." Talking to a reporter "from his rostrum, the bootblack stand in the County Court-house," the redoubtable Tammany figure allowed as how the Irishman's "one thought is to serve the city which gave him a home." No doubt with a twinkle in his eye, Plunkitt went on: "He has this thought even before he lands in New York, for his friends here often have a good place in one of the city departments picked out for him while he is still in the old country. Is it any wonder that he has a tender spot in his heart for old New York when he is on its salary list the mornin' after he lands?" [6]

The "once unwelcome Irishman" was also capable of

victimizing others as he had been victimized, as the famed journalist and social reformer Jacob Riis reported in 1890. In describing what was happening to the Italians, Russian Jews, and Chinese who followed the Irish into New York's slums, Riis found the Irishman "picturesquely autocratic" as a landlord, "an apt pupil" who was "merely showing forth the result of the schooling he had received, reenacting, in his own way, the scheme of the tenements." It was "only his frankness that shocks." [7]

In addition, the Irish most emphatically brought along their disdain for pomp and circumstance, something that was, of course, very American. The Irish had their own particular way of deflating the pompous with mischievous mockery, sarcasm, and tongue-in-cheek humor. The Irish put their adversary off by putting him on.

They did it from the time of their arrival, applying an old-country style to a New World of fragile status, yearning ambition, and social pretensions. It was their effective technique for turning the tables on the powerful without actually confronting their power. The ultimate example of this style was "Martin Dooley"—a bachelor, a saloonkeeper, and a Roscommon Irishman. He looked out at the Irish-American scene, at politics and power, and at man's passing vanities with characteristic Irish wit and wisdom. He wreaked humorous havoc as a national jester, a wise, biting critic disguised as a clown who twitted American foibles much as the Irishman back home twitted the Englishman. Mr. Dooley was actually Finley Peter Dunne, a Chicago newspaperman, who created the character in 1893 to say what Dunne himself could not say directly. With the help of a slow-witted straight man named Hennessy, Dooley's satirical monologues caught national attention in widely-syndicated newspaper sketches and in a series of books.

Dunne spelled out his strategy in *Mr. Dooley At His Best*, a collection dedicated to "The Hennessys of the World Who Suffer and Are Silent." Mr. Dooley was originally called "Col. McNeery," but the name was changed when his real-life inspiration and Dunne's favorite saloonkeeper, Jim McGarry, became enraged at the ridicule he faced from his friends. After some light-hearted "Col. McNeery" sketches, Dunne conscripted him to serve in a newspaper crusade against civic corruption. It occurred to Dunne that "while it might be dangerous to call an alderman a thief in English no one could sue if a comic Irishman denounced the statesman as a thief." So "Col. McNeery" was used "to bludgeon the bribe-taking members of the council." The outcome, Dunne reports, was that the "crooks were ridiculed by their friends who delighted in reading these articles aloud in public places." Dunne thereby linked himself to an Irish comic tradition: "If I had written the same thing in English I would inevitably have been pistolled or slugged, as other critics were. But my victims did not dare to complain. They felt bound to smile and treat these highly libelous articles as mere humorous skits." [8]

Mr. Dooley's commentaries were at the heart of Irish-Americanism, a sense of *vanitas vanitatum*, an absorption in everyday trivia and a sense of its triviality. The optimism of the creator of Mr. Dooley was, his son wrote, "streaked with cynicism and fatalism, as became a son of Ireland." [9] Irish humor, through mockery, parody, and satire, kept a sense of balance, a large pin to prick bloated exaggerations and blind faith. For as Mr. Dooley said, "there's somethin' th' matther with ivry man, an' if there wasn't he'd be lynched." [10]

Literary critic Vivian Mercier has shown in a scholarly work, *The Irish Comic Tradition*, how reverence and ridicule run together in Irish literature. It is as if the Irish have always tried to protect themselves from going too far. Mercier notes that "the figure of the sceptic and/or parodist" lurks "behind the bards and hagiographers, who endlessly strive to outdo each

other in their accounts of heroic deeds and saintly miracles."
In the end, Mercier concludes that "no aspect of life is too
sacred to escape the mockery of Irish laughter." [11]

In rummaging through the Irish immigrant newspapers and
books by and about the Irish in America, examples of sarcasm
and mockery abound, though they do not always wear well.
When, for example, the *Boston Pilot* wanted to put down a
rival Methodist newspaper called *The Olive Branch*, the *Pilot*'s
editorial exclaimed: "The editors of this paper have given it a
funny name. If it were called the Spit Fire now, or the
Hornet's Nest, or any name betokening an itch for worrying
people, and putting them out of humor with themselves and
with every body else, the thing must pass. The *Olive Branch*
indeed! We wonder if the senior or the junior ever held out the
Olive Branch to any one?" [12]

Or, as told with relish by the *New Orleans Crescent*, an
Irishman was repairing a telegraph wire when an "Exquisite"
came along and asked in a condescending accent whether the
storm had broken the wire. No, was the answer. The lightning?
No. Then the answer: "The fact is, sur, that a missage was sint
on from New York, about the sale of a cargo of lead—lead, you
know, is very heavy intirely, sur—and be gor, the weight of it
broke the wire, as you can see, into smidereens!" When the
"snob" noted that it was a very remarkable fact, " 'pon my
'oneau," the Irishman replied with "a roguish leer," "it would
be more so, if it wasn't—like the estates of some of the
discindents of the ould Irish Kings—founded on fancy!" [13]

The *Providence* [R.I.] *Telegram* reported what happened
when a mill owner urged his Irish worker not to vote for the
Democratic Party. "Pat, don't you vote for the Democratic
Ticket," the employer said. "It is a free trade ticket. If that
party wins, your wages will be reduced one-half." To which
Pat replied: "Divil trust ye now. If that's so, ye'd vote for it
yourself." [14]

In post-Civil War New York, a visiting Englishwoman called

on a friend and asked the Irish servant if his "mistress was at home." As noted by John White in his *Sketches from America*, no American dared "speak of the 'master' or 'mistress' of a household," such terms having gone out with slavery. Thus the Irishman at the door replied with courtesy and a straight face: "No ma'am, the fact is, I don't keep one at present." [15]

As for the Know-Nothings, there was Mrs. Quigg's reply when asked if her husband were one: "I guess so, for he told me this morning that somebody had been making a fool of him." Or "The Last Yankee Cry—No English! no Irish! no Germans! no taxes! no government! no babies! know-nothings!"

For the Irish, ridicule was a way to cut others down to size, whether strangers, neighbors, or members of the family. Putting on airs was clearly an Irish temptation that called for deflation. Versifying on "The Passing of Pat," Nancy McCready noted that he was "sure a fine man"—"him always just and fair even if he was given to puttin on airs." To cut others down to size, "taking the mickey" or "having a crack" (ridicule) was called for.

Inside the family, a rough warmth and a tough tenderness prevailed. Playwright William Alfred notes that there were nicknames to someone's face, nicknames behind his back, and a "tortuous" show of affection: "Martin was called Mutton as well as Mortyeen Hungry Jaws; William was called Wally to his face, and the more malicious Miggsy behind his back ('Miggs!' is what you cried, holding your thumbs, when you had the misfortune of meeting a person with cockeyes).

"The tortuousness of the show of affection generally underlying the choice of these epithets always seemed to me to spring from the bleak Irish terror of 'overlooking' those one admired, of giving them, that is, the evil eye, calling the Devil's attention to them by imprudent praise. Love was never easily expressed in word or gesture. Kissing and hugging were as dangerous as they were vulgar. Honey, darling, sweetheart, and dear were words clowns used in books. In the family, they would have raised hoots of derision. 'You' was the most intimate form of address. It could be used with crippling fury or devastating tenderness." [16]

From poetic flights of Irish literature to rough working-man's responses, from the syndicated "Mr. Dooley" to the tough tenderness of family life, Irish-Americans created a popular image and also suffered a social liability as they entered the twentieth century. They were still not socially accepted, particularly in Boston. As Thomas Beer reported in his much-quoted account of American life at the end of the nineteenth century, the Irish "were at once established as tremendously funny, gay and charming people and concurrently were snubbed." [17]

That snubbing burned. It contributed to Irish militancy in the social arena as the cause of Irish freedom had fired them politically. Quietly but surely, Irish-Americans launched a strong drive toward respectability. One of the earlier accounts of this drive emerged from a flowery, self-serving chronicle of travel among Irish-Americans in the 1850's by Jeremiah O'Donovan. He was out peddling his own published writings, including an Irish history in epic verse, and wrote of encounters with his countrymen. ("No glowing eloquence, no sublimity of thought, no lofty aspirations, or no meretricious ornament can have any analogy with the brief sketch of my travels. . . .") [18]

O'Donovan filled the account of his travels in America with flattering descriptions of his hosts and potential customers. What came through again and again were images of much-desired respectability. In Philadelphia, Roger Brown the grocer was "generous, hospitable, kind, consoling, facetious, agreeable, learned, and strictly honest in all his dealings and social intercourse. . . . Mr. McNamara kept a respectable inn in Brooklyn . . . a gentleman indeed, in principle and practice. . . . Messr. Henry & Poland (of Cincinnati) cannot be excelled in honor, honesty and industry, and indisputably in fair dealing. . . . Miss O'Donovan (who helped her brother-in-law run a New York grocery) is young, beautiful, prudent, religious, and incontrovertibly honest . . . Mr. James Laughlin, plumber . . . and his lady (of New York) are indisputably clever, kind, affectionate and patriotic; they are very popular and bear truly irreproachable characters." [19]

An Irish-born playwright named Dion Boucicault, whose plays were American hits in the second half of the nineteenth century, watched as Irish-Americans aspired to high social standing and were turned back. In one letter, written from New York in 1877, he noted that he had "heard a great deal too much of humiliating slights put upon Irish ladies at balls and there are rules against us at one of the best clubs in town." He found that the Emmets were "the one Irish family who had entrée everywhere." A short time before his death in 1890 Boucicault advised an Irish-American who complained that his wife had been snubbed to go West and change his name.[20]

From all accounts, social striving became an important preoccupation of the Irish-American families who were succeeding in all other ways. In his account of the Irish-American rich, author Stephen Birmingham has contrasted them with American Jews, whose wealthy elite he has also chronicled. Whereas American Jews kept to themselves and tended to shun "society," Birmingham describes the Irish hunger for social recognition, for notices in society columns, and for listings in social registers, for "America's emergent Irish families were proving themselves a socially ambitious lot." [21]

The sensitivity to social snubbing lingered on, even for a Kennedy in a chauffeur-driven limousine. Mrs. Rose Kennedy, the daughter of the first Irish-born mayor of Boston (John "Honey Fitz" Fitzgerald) and wife of tycoon Joseph P. Kennedy, was driving her son John and a classmate from Harvard to New York during a college holiday. When she heard the classmate's name and recognized him as a member of a leading Boston family, she turned suddenly to him "with a note of desperation in her voice" and blurted: "Tell me, when are the nice people of Boston going to accept us?" [22]

For the most part, whether they were F.I.F.'s (First Irish Families, which the Kennedys were not) or lace curtain, Irish-Americans did not abandon their identity while pursuing social recognition. Thus, in New York, Boston, and elsewhere, they did socially what they always did politically. They remained Irish and they knocked hard on the door to be let in.

In establishing their place in America, the Irish insisted that devotion to the old country did not conflict with their Americanism. A literature of justification, underscored by lectures and speeches, proliferated. Irish-Americans stressed their role in the American Revolution and their unwavering loyalty to the Republic, adding their contribution to the country's spectacular economic growth. Irish-American apologists, such as Thomas D'Arcy McGee, provided historical counterarguments for critics so that Irish-Americans could say with justification: "This is our country, too. We bought our place dearly." McGee's widely-publicized lectures appeared in two books much favored by nineteenth-century Irish-Americans: *History of the Irish Settlers in North America* (1851) and *The Catholic History of North America* (1855). At the same time, Irish-Americans linked support of Irish nationalism to the ideals of a nation that had won its own independence by rebelling against England. As the *Irish World* proclaimed on the one-hundredth anniversary of the American Revolution: "The cause of America in 1776 is the cause of Ireland in 1876."

Early in the twentieth century, Irish consciousness grew even stronger as the United States moved toward alliance with England against Germany. Militant Irish-Americans and German-Americans demanded that America remain neutral as Europe headed toward war, the former out of hostility for England, the latter out of sympathy for Germany. Irish-

Americans were never more Irish. Weekly newspapers were launched to foster "Irish national needs" as lecturers arrived from Ireland to discourse on Irish history and poetry before audiences from Boston to Butte, Montana. Irish-Americans turned out to applaud plays about Irish nationalism, bought books about heroes in Ireland's fight for freedom and grew misty-eyed at the sound of Irish music. All this was further stimulated by the short-lived heroics of the 1916 Easter Rebellion in Dublin, which failed abysmally as a rebellion but once again supplied martyrs for the American Irish, who, in turn, had supplied aid to the rebels. A historian sympathetic to Irish nationalism has noted of those years that "the anthem of Ireland had many American notes." [23]

In America, the hyphen in the Irish-American identity became a troublesome issue, once again arousing Irish feelings of oppression. Their loyalty was questioned, even to the extent that U.S. Secret Service agents attended meetings of Irish-American organizations. Provocation had come from the top when President Woodrow Wilson inflamed Irish-Americans by casting doubts on their patriotism. In May, 1914, while dedicating a monument to John Barry, the Irish-American naval hero of the American Revolution, Wilson pointedly described Barry as an Irishman whose "heart crossed the Atlantic with him." The implication was that contemporary Irish-Americans (and German-Americans, too) did not have their hearts all in one place. He made his point even clearer by referring to Americans who "need hyphens in their names, because only part of them has come over" (Wilson conveniently omitted the other half of the equation: that only part of them was accepted when they did come over).

The tempest concerning "hyphenism" carried over into the Presidential campaign of 1916, but once America entered the war in April, 1917, loyalty won out quickly and dramatically. "Contrary to earlier, gloomy predictions," historian Wittke has pointed out, "the hyphen dissolved in the heat of war.

Government officials from the President down testified repeatedly to the loyalty of the foreign-born." [24]

At the height of the "hyphenism" furor, the position of Irish-Americans was well-stated by a secondary headline over a lengthy article in Walt Whitman's old newspaper, *The Brooklyn Eagle*: TO CALL THE MEMBERS OF THE HIBERNIAN RACE FOREIGNERS WOULD BE AN ANOMALY, AS THEY ARE AN INTEGRAL PART OF AMERICANISM. The Irish, said the lengthy article, "have become an integral part of us, and even those of us who may be descended from the passengers of the Mayflower can hardly look upon them as foreigners. Once here, the Irish have bound us so closely to that little isle whence they came that we no longer look upon Ireland as a foreign country. . . . Everyone in the United States knows that the 'Old Country' can refer only to the Emerald Isle, and every American audience of non-Hibernian extraction is stirred by Irish songs and allusions to Ireland. It has become a very part of us. We feel that, after the United States, Ireland is the country in which we take the most interest. This very remarkable psychological state is due entirely to the Irishman's wonderfully passionate patriotism. . . . But the Irishman's love for his old home has never made him relegate America to second place." [25]

German-Americans, like Irish-Americans, demonstrated their loyalty and patriotism during World War I, but at a much higher cost to their hyphenated identity. Because of their identification with the enemy power, German-Americans were subjected to a brief and bizarre hate campaign with the coming of World War I. There was a drive against German music, literature, singing societies, language in the schools, and music in concert programs. There were anti-sauerkraut and anti-Dachshund campaigns. Hamburgers were renamed "Salisbury Steaks" and sauerkraut "Liberty Cabbage." There was mob violence as well and it was a time for changing names—from Schmidt to Smith, from Muller to Miller, from

Schwarz to Black. In his history of German-Americans, Richard O'Connor sums up: "Within the hours it took to bring the United States into the war, German-Americanism disappeared forever." [26]

Not so at all with the Irish. They fought enthusiastically to make the world—including Ireland—safe for democracy. Irish-Americans agitated for self-determination for Ireland and, as President Wilson prepared to leave for the Versailles Conference, they stepped up their campaign for Irish freedom. The high point came at New York's Madison Square Garden on December 10, 1918, when Boston's Cardinal O'Connell addressed an emotion-charged meeting organized by the Friends of Irish Freedom. The arena was overflowing with Irish-American enthusiasts who heard what they wanted to hear and what they wanted President Wilson to heed: "This war, we were told again and again by all those responsible for the conduct of the war, was for justice for all, for the inviolable rights of small nations, for the inalienable right, inherent in every nation, of self-determination. The purpose of this meeting tonight is very specific. The war can only be justified by the universal application of those principles. Let that application begin with Ireland." [27]

That Wilson did not heed their wishes at Versailles, but that Ireland did officially gain its freedom in January, 1922, were international dimensions of the Irish-American reality. In the United States, the Irish had developed a distinctive identity. They were determined to retain their Irishness (including their Catholicism) and they were determined to be accepted as Americans. They were neither willing nor able to give up either half of their identity as they evolved from despised new arrivals to powerful political and religious activists. They yielded to no one in being either Irish or American.

In the period of American history stretching from the Famine Migration to a return to Europe as part of an American Expeditionary Force in World War I, the Irish maintained their pattern. Through slum, saloon, and sandbag to mansion and cathedral, from poverty to power, they held to their double identity, shaping and being shaped by the American experience. Thus entered the Irish-American.

Notes

Introduction

1. John F. Kennedy, *A Nation of Immigrants* (New York: Harper & Row, 1964), p. 68.
2. Oscar Handlin, *The Uprooted* (New York: Grosset's Universal Library, 1957), p. 3. Originally published in 1951 by Little, Brown and Company.
3. Samuel Griswold Goodrich, quoted in Edith Abbott, *Historical Aspects of the Immigration Problem: Select Documents* (Chicago: University of Chicago Press, 1926), p. 741.
4. Quoted in Florence E. Gibson, *The Attitudes of the New York Irish Toward State and National Affairs, 1848–1892* (New York: Columbia University Press, 1951), p. 15.
5. Quoted in *Boston Pilot*, July 1, 1854.
6. William Chambers, *Things As They Are in America* (London, 1854), p. 352.

7. *The Diary of George Templeton Strong*, Allan Nevins and Milton Halsey Thomas, eds. (New York: Macmillan Co., 1952), vol. III, pp. 342–343.

8. Jeremiah O'Donovan, *Travels in America, 1854–55* (Pittsburgh, Pa., 1864), p. 4.

9. Quoted in Thomas Beer, *The Mauve Decade* (New York: Alfred A. Knopf, 1926), p. 153.

10. Finley Peter Dunne, *Mr. Dooley on Making A Will and Other Necessary Evils* (New York: Charles Scribner's Sons, 1919), pp. 196–197.

Chapter I

1. Carl Wittke, *The Irish in America* (Baton Rouge: Louisiana State University Press, 1956), p. 4.

2. Andrew M. Greeley, *That Most Distressful Nation* (Chicago: Quadrangle Books, 1972), p. 27.

3. Quoted in Giovanni Costigan, *A History of Modern Ireland* (New York: Pegasus, 1970), p. 94.

4. Quoted in George Potter, *To the Golden Door: The Story of the Irish in Ireland and America* (Boston: Little, Brown and Company, 1960), pp. 34, 39.

5. Quoted in Abbott, *op. cit.*, p. 254.

6. Quoted in *ibid.*, p. 101.

7. Cecil Woodham-Smith, *The Reason Why* (New York: E. P. Dutton & Co. paperback, 1960), p. 112.

8. *Ibid.*

9. Quoted in Abbott, *op. cit.*, pp. 116–117.

10. Quoted in Potter, *op. cit.*, p. 48.

11. Quoted in *The Great Famine*, R. Dudley Edwards and T. Desmond Williams, eds. (New York: New York University Press, 1957), pp. 232–233.

12. Quoted in Oscar Handlin, *Boston's Immigrants* (New York: Atheneum paperback, 1970), pp. 45–46.

13. Quoted in *ibid.*, p. 47.

14. Arnold Schrier, *Ireland and the American Emigration, 1850–1900* (Minneapolis: University of Minnesota Press, 1958), p. 10.

15. Quoted in *ibid.*, p. 40.
16. *Ibid.*, p. 175. Based on his study of a cross-section of emigrant letters to Ireland, Arnold Schrier set forth the "usual opening sentence."
17. Quoted in Potter, *op. cit.*, pp. 129–130.
18 "Letter of John Doyle," *Journal of the American Irish Historical Society*, vol. XII (1912–1913), pp. 197–204.
19. Quoted in Leonard Wibberly, *The Coming of the Green* (New York: Hold, 1958), p. 7.
20. Quoted in Marcus L. Hansen, "Immigration and Puritanism," Norwegian-American Studies and Records, vol. IX, p. 11.
21. Quoted in Potter, *op. cit.*, p. 166.

Chapter II

1. Conrad Arensberg, *The Irish Countryman* (Garden City, New York: Natural History Press, 1968), p. 191. Originally published in 1937.
2. Harriet Martineau, *Letters from Ireland* (London, 1852), p. 11.
3. Quoted in Potter, *op. cit.*, p. 157.
4. William Alfred, "Pride and Poverty," in *The Immigrant Experience*, Thomas C. Wheeler, ed. (New York: Dial Press, 1971), p. 20.
5. Quoted in Terry Coleman, *Going to America* (New York: Pantheon Books, 1972), p. 75.
6. John Francis Maguire, *The Irish in America* (London, 1868), pp. 179–181.
7. Quoted in Edwin C. Guillet, *The Great Migration* (Toronto: University of Toronto Press, 1963), pp. 96–97. Originally published in 1937.
8. Thomas Colley Grattan, *Civilized America* (London, 1859), p. 5.

Chapter III

1. Quoted in Guillet, *op. cit.*, pp. 185–186.
2. Quoted in Abbott, *op. cit.*, pp. 227–228.

3. Maguire, *op. cit.*, pp. 190–192.
4. Alfred E. Smith, *Up To Now* (New York: Viking Press, 1929), p. 3.
5. Quoted in Potter, *op. cit.*, p. 167.
6. Philip H. Bagenal, *The American Irish and Their Influence on Irish Politics* (Boston: Roberts Brothers, 1882), p. 73.
7. Quoted in Abbott, *op. cit.*, pp. 635, 637.
8. Quoted in Maguire, *op. cit.*, p. 220.
9. Quoted in Maguire, *op. cit.*, pp. 223–225.
10. Bagenal, *op. cit.*, p. 72.
11. Quoted in Abbott, *op. cit.*, pp. 594–595.
12. Maguire, *op. cit.*, p. 186.
13. Handlin, *Boston's Immigrants, op. cit.*, p. 118.
14. Quoted in Maguire, *op. cit.*, p. 228.

Chapter IV

1. Dr. Cahill, "Seventh Letter from America," *Boston Pilot*, March 3, 1860.
2. Handlin, *Boston's Immigrants, op. cit.*, pp. 57–60.
3. Bagenal, *op. cit.*, pp. 68–70.
4. *The Diary of George Templeton Strong, op. cit.*, vol. II, p. 348.
5. Document 37 in Abbott, *op. cit.*, p. 832.
6. Rev. M. B. Buckley, *Diary of A Tour In America* (Dublin, 1886), p. 142.
7. Quoted in Maguire, *op. cit.*, p. 337.
8. John White, *Sketches from America* (London, 1870), p. 371.
9. Quoted in *New York Tribune*, November 10, 1851.
10. Edward Robb Ellis, *The Epic of New York City* (New York: Coward-McCann, 1966), p. 248–249.
11. Grattan, *op. cit.*, p. 30.
12. Maguire, *op. cit.*, p. 284–285.
13. James D. Burn, *Three Years Among the Working Classes During the Civil War* (London, 1865), pp. 14–15.
14. Quoted in Edward M. Levine, *The Irish and Irish Politicians* (Notre Dame, Indiana: University of Notre Dame Press, 1966), pp. 117–118.

15. J. L. Spalding, *Religious Mission of the Irish People* (New York: Christian Press Association Publishing Co., 1880), pp. 106–108.
16. Quoted in W. F. Adams, *Ireland and the Irish Emigration to the New World* (New York: Russell & Russell, 1932), p. 342.
17. Document 99 in *Documents of American Catholic History*, John Tracy Ellis, ed. (Milwaukee: Bruce Publishing Co., 1956), p. 329.
18. Spalding, *op. cit.*, p. 147.
19. Maguire, *op. cit.*, p. 262.

Chapter V

1. Quoted in John Henry Cutler, *"Honey Fitz"*: *The Colorful Life and Times of John F. ("Honey Fitz") Fitzgerald* (Indianapolis: Bobbs-Merrill, 1962), p. 22.
2. *Life and Letters of Edwin Lawrence Godkin* (New York: Macmillan, 1907), vol. I, pp. 181–184.
3. Earl F. Niehaus, *The Irish in New Orleans* (Baton Rouge: Louisiana State University Press, 1965), p. 129.
4. Mrs. M. C. J. F. Houstoun, *Hesperos* (London, 1850), vol. I, p. 179. Cited by Max Berger in "The Irish Emigrant and American Nativism," *The Pennsylvania Magazine*, April, 1946, vol. LXX, no. 2, p. 148.
5. Quoted in Peter Guilday, *The Life and Times of John England* (New York: The America Press, 1927), vol. I, p. 365.
6. Henry De Courcy and John Gilmary Shea, *History of the Catholic Church in the United States* (New York: P. J. Kenedy, 1896), pp. 239–240.
7. William Cardinal O'Connell, *Recollections of Seventy Years* (Boston: Houghton Mifflin Co., 1934), pp. 5–6.
8. Ray Allen Billington, *The Protestant Crusade, 1800–1860* (New York: Macmillan Co., 1938), p. 367.
9. *Documents Relating to the Ursuline Convent in Charlestown* . . . (1842), pp. 13–14. Quoted in *American Violence: A Documentary History*, Richard Hofstadter and Michael Wallace, eds. (New York: Random House, Vintage Books, 1971), pp. 300–301.

10. "The Anti-Catholic Riots in Philadelphia in 1844," *American Catholic Historical Researches*, vol. XIII (April, 1896), pp. 60–61.
11. John R. G. Hassard, *Life of the Most Rev. John Hughes* (New York: Appleton & Co., 1866), pp. 276–278.
12. Quoted in *Boston Catholic Observer*, November 8–15, 1848.

Chapter VI

1. Thomas Sugrue, *A Catholic Speaks His Mind on America's Religious Conflict* (New York: Harper, 1951), p. 42.
2. For an examination of the pressures facing Irish Catholicism and American Catholicism in general in the wake of the Second Vatican Council, see Edward Wakin and Father Joseph F. Scheuer, *The De-Romanization of the American Catholic Church* (New York: Macmillan, 1966).
3. Spalding, *op. cit.*, p. 62.
4. Thomas N. Brown, *Irish-American Nationalism, 1870–1890* (Philadelphia: J. B. Lippincott Co., 1966), p. 34.
5. James Jeffrey Roche, *Life of John Boyle O'Reilly* (New York: Mershon Company, 1891), p. 377.
6. Nathan Glazer and Daniel Patrick Moynihan, *Beyond the Melting Pot* (Cambridge, Mass.: M.I.T. Press and Harvard University Press, 1963), p. 230.
7. Potter, *op. cit.*, p. 344.
8. Quoted in *ibid.*, p. 356.
9. Document 98 in *Documents of American Catholic History, op. cit.*, p. 313.
10. *Ibid.*, p. 421.
11. Annals of the Sisters of Mercy, pp. 193–194, quoted in Henry W. Casper, SJ, *History of the Catholic Church in Nebraska* (Milwaukee: Bruce Publishing Co., 1966), pp. 66–67.
12. Maguire, *op. cit.*, p. 338.
13. O'Connell, *op. cit.*, p. 2.
14. Rose Fitzgerald Kennedy, *Times to Remember* (Garden City, N.Y.: Doubleday & Co., 1974), p. 14.

15. Maguire, *op. cit.*, p. 558.
16. *Ibid.*, pp. 558–559.
17. Quoted in *Progress of the Catholic Church in America and the Great Columbian Catholic Congress of 1893* (Chicago: J. S. Hyland Co., 1897), p. 449.
18. James D. McCabe, *Lights and Shadows of New York Life: Or Sights and Sensations of the Great City* (Philadelphia: National Publishing Co., 1872), p. 449.
19. James Parton, "Our Roman Catholic Brethren," *The Atlantic Monthly*, April, 1898, p. 434.
20. Quoted in Hassard, *op. cit.*, pp. 80–81.
21. Quoted in Beer, *op. cit.*, pp. 157–158.
22. Spalding, *op. cit.*, pp. 136–137.
23. Theodore Maynard, *The Story of American Catholicism* (New York: The Macmillan Company, 1942), p. 550.

Chapter VII

1. Thomas L. Nichols, *Forty Years of American Life* (London, 1864), vol. II, p. 68.
2. *Boston Pilot*, September 24, 1836.
3. Bagenal, *op. cit.*, p. 40.
4. Quoted in Potter, *op. cit.*, p. 229.
5. Finley Peter Dunne, *Mr. Dooley's Opinions* (New York: R. H. Russell, 1901), pp. 171–172.
6. *The Leader*, December 12, 1865.
7. Quoted in Document 7, p. 438, Abbott, *op. cit.* Excerpted from Francis Lieber, *The Stranger in America* (London, 1835).
8. *New York Tribune*, November 26, 1867.
9. Quoted in Gibson, *op. cit.*, p. 390.
10. *New York Tribune*, July 29, 1884.
11. *Irish American*, July 28, 1884.
12. Edward A. Ross, *The Old World in the New* (New York: The Century Co., 1914), p. 261.
13. William V. Shannon, *The American Irish* (New York: Macmillan Co., 1960), p. 401.
14. Levine, *op. cit.*, p. 129.

15. Wittke, *op. cit.*, p. 103.
16. *Ibid.*, p. 112.
17. *New York Sun*, August 9, 1875.
18. Lincoln Steffens, *Autobiography* (New York: Harcourt, Brace, 1931), p. 618.
19. Quoted in Cutler, *op. cit.*, p. 50.
20. Kennedy, *op. cit.*, pp. 20–21.
21. J. Frank Kernan, *Reminiscences of the Old Fire Laddies and Fire Departments of New York and Brooklyn* (New York, 1885), p. 49.
22. Smith, *op. cit.*, pp. 32–33.
23. Frances Perkins, *The Roosevelt I Knew* (New York: Viking Press, 1946), p. 14.
24. Wittke, *op. cit.*, p. 112.
25. Steffens, *op. cit.*, pp. 236–238.
26. *New York Tribune*, October 17, 1866.
27. *New York Times*, May 2, 1878.
28. *New York Times*, May 6, 1878.

Chapter VIII

1. Quoted in Wittke, *op. cit.*, p. 138.
2. Quoted in Paul Jones, *The Irish Brigade* (Washington-New York: Robert B. Luce, Inc., 1969), p. 100.
3. Quoted in Potter, *op. cit.*, p. 622.
4. David P. Conyngham, *The Irish Brigade and Its Campaigns* (New York, 1867), pp. 5–6.
5. Quoted in *New York Herald*, October 8, 1861.
6. Michael Cavanagh, *Memoirs of Gen. Thomas Francis Meagher* (Worcester, Mass., 1892), pp. 373–375.
7. *Boston Transcript*, October 3, 1861.
8. Lloyd Lewis, *Sherman: Fighting Prophet* (New York: Harcourt, Brace, 1932), p. 176.
9. Quoted in Handlin, *Boston's Immigrants, op. cit.*, p. 210.
10. Leonard Wibberley, *The Coming of the Green* (New York: Henry Holt and Company, 1958), pp. 78–79.
11. Jones, *op. cit.*, p. 85.
12. Quoted in *ibid.*, p. 89.

13. Quoted in Cavanagh, *op. cit.*, pp. 446–447.
14. Quoted in *ibid.*, p. 460.
15. Quoted in *ibid.*, pp. 461–462.
16. Quoted in *ibid.*, pp. 470–471.
17. Quoted in Conyngham, *op. cit.*, pp. 351–352.
18. Quoted in Cavanagh, *op. cit.*, p. 470.
19. Quoted in Wibberley, *op. cit.*, p. 78.
20. Letter from Patrick Dunny to his father, brothers, and sister, October 22, 1861, Philadelphia. Quoted in Schrier, *op. cit.*, p. 178.
21. *American Violence: A Documentary History, op. cit.*, p. 211.
22. Quoted in Wittke, *op. cit.*, p. 144.
23. Quoted in *New York Tribune*, July 18, 1863.
24. *American Violence: A Documentary History, op. cit.*, p. 212.
25. *Harper's Weekly*, August 1, 1863.
26. Shannon, *op. cit.*, pp. 57–58.
27. Beer, *op. cit.*, pp. 152–153.
28. Francis P. Duffy, *Father Duffy's Story* (New York: George H. Doran Company, 1919), p. 14.
29. Quoted in Ella M. E. Flick, *Chaplain Duffy of the Sixty-Ninth Regiment* (Philadelphia: Dolphin Press, 1935), p. 166.
30. Quoted in Corey Ford, *Donovan of O.S.S.* (Boston: Little, Brown and Company, 1970), p. 32.
31. *New York Sun*, April 29, 1919.

Chapter IX

1. *Irish-American Almanac* for 1875 (New York, 1874), p. 30.
2. Cecil Woodham-Smith, *The Great Hunger* (London: New English Library paperback edition, 1970), p. 409.
3. Maguire, *op. cit.*, pp. 598–601.
4. Charles Mackay, *Life and Liberty in America* (New York, 1859), pp. 112–113.
5. Elizabeth Gurley Flynn, *I Speak My Own Piece* (New York: Masses and Mainstream, 1955), p. 13.
6. Quoted in Potter, *op. cit.*, pp. 396–398.
7. Quoted in Cavanagh, *op. cit.*, p. 353.

8. *Ibid.*, p. 443.
9. Quoted in *New York Herald*, January 26, 1866.
10. Wittke, *op. cit.*, p. 150.
11. William D'Arcy, O.F.M. Conv., *The Fenian Movement in the United States: 1858–1886* (Washington, D.C.: Catholic University of America Press, 1947), p. 164.
12. *New York Times*, May 29, 1870.
13. Quoted in D'Arcy, *op. cit.*, p. 371.
14. Wittke, *op. cit.*, p. 47.
15. Joel Tyler Headley, *The Great Riots of New York: 1712–1873* (Indianapolis: Bobbs-Merrill Co., 1970), pp. 290–293. First published by E. B. Treat, New York, 1873.
16. Quoted in *American Violence: A Documentary History, op. cit.*, p. 321.
17. Headley, *op. cit.*, pp. 301–303.
18. *Boston Pilot*, July 29, 1871, quoted by James Jeffrey Roche in *Life of John Boyle O'Reilly* (New York: Mershon Co., 1891), pp. 118–119.
19. Brown, *op. cit.*, p. 46.
20. *Ibid.*, p. 47.
21. Quoted in Katherine Murray, "Voluntary Associations Among Irish-Americans," unpublished master's thesis, Catholic University, Washington, D.C., 1967.
22. Sister Martha Julie Keehan, "The Irish Catholic Beneficial Societies Founded Between 1818 and 1869," Ph.D. thesis, Catholic University of America, Washington, D.C., 1953, pp. 34–35.
23. *Irish World*, September 3, 1892.
24. John D. Crimmins, *St. Patrick's Day: Its Celebration in New York and Other American Places, 1737–1845*. Published by the author, New York, 1902, pp. 13–14.
25. *Ibid.*, p. 22.
26. *New York Times*, March 17, 1870.
27. Dunne, *Mr. Dooley's Opinions, op. cit.*, pp. 189–190.

Chapter X

1. Quoted in *Makers of America—The New Immigrants, 1904–13*, Wayne Moquin, ed. (Encyclopaedia Britannica Educational Corporation, 1971), vol. VI, pp. 180–181.

2. Brown, *op. cit.*, p. 133.

3. Chambers, *op. cit.*, p. 352.

4. Shannon, *op. cit.*, p. 136.

5. Harry Golden, "East Side Memoir, 1910's" in *Autobiographies of American Jews*, Harold U. Ribalow, ed. (Philadelphia: Jewish Publication Society of America, 1965), p. 310.

6. William L. Reardon, *Plunkitt of Tammany Hall* (New York, 1905), pp. 58–59.

7. Jacob Riis, *How the Other Half Lives* (Cambridge, Mass.: Harvard University Press, 1970), pp. 18–19. Originally published in 1890.

8. Finley Peter Dunne, *Mr. Dooley At His Best* (New York: Charles Scribner's Sons, 1938), p. xxiii.

9. "Commentary" by Philip Dunne in Finley Peter Dunne, *Mr. Dooley Remembers* (Boston: Little Brown and Company, 1963), p. 216.

10. Finley Peter Dunne, *Mr. Dooley On Making A Will and Other Necessary Evils*, *op. cit.*, p. 25.

11. Vivian Mercier, *The Irish Comic Tradition* (Oxford: Oxford University Press, 1962), pp. 12, 248.

12. *Boston Pilot*, August 3, 1850.

13. Quoted in *Boston Pilot*, April 27, 1850.

14. Quoted in *Boston Pilot*, February 25, 1888.

15. John White, *Sketches from America* (London, 1870), p. 371.

16. Alfred, *op. cit.*, p. 28.

17. Beer, *op. cit.*, p. 152.

18. O'Donovan, *op. cit.*, p. 7.

19. O'Donovan, *op. cit.*, pp. 138, 97, 354, 161–162.

20. Quoted in Beer, *op. cit.*, p. 150.

21. Stephen Birmingham, *Real Lace* (New York: Harper & Row, 1973), p. 39.

22. Quoted in Birmingham, *op. cit.*, p. 186.
23. Charles Callan Tansill, *America and the Fight for Irish Freedom, 1866–1922* (New York: Devin-Adair Co., 1957), p. 135.
24. Wittke, *op. cit.*, p. 283.
25. *Brooklyn Eagle*, March 19, 1916.
26. Richard O'Connor, *The German-Americans* (Boston: Little Brown and Company, 1968), p. 413.
27. Quoted in Tansill, *op. cit.*, p. 280.

Index

183